The little CURRY cookbook

The little CURRY cookbook

MURDOCH BOOKS
SYDNEY · LONDON

CONTENTS

INTRODUCTION ◌◌◌ 6

RICH CURRY ◌◌◌ 12

EARTHY CURRY ◌◌◌ 40

FOOD JOURNEY: BREADS ◌◌◌ 58

HOT AND SOUR ◌◌◌ 80

AROMATIC ◌◌◌ 108

FOOD JOURNEY: SPICES ◌◌◌ 126

SOFTLY SWEET ◌◌◌ 148

FOOD JOURNEY: RICE ◌◌◌ 164

BASICS ◌◌◌ 180

GLOSSARY ◌◌◌ 188

INDEX ◌◌◌ 190

BRING ALIVE THE FLAVOURS OF CURRIES:
RICH, EARTHY, HOT AND SOUR, AROMATIC, OR
SOFTLY SWEET. INFUSED WITH FRESH, LEAFY
HERBS AND FRAGRANT SPICES, CURRIES ARE
MUCH MORE THAN SIMPLY 'HOT' OR 'SPICY'.

For such a humble sounding word, 'curry' refers to some of the world's most delicious and popular dishes. The word itself was first coined by the British in India, possibly deriving from the Tamil word kari, meaning 'spiced sauce'. Today the term covers dishes that range from simple to sophisticated, complex to singularly bold, those that can be made in minutes or left for hours over a bed of coals, and includes the everyday food of peasants to the once-exclusive creations of the rich and royal.

Use of the word has expanded to include the curries of Southeast Asia alongside those of India, and this book features dishes from cuisines as varied as those of Kashmir, Goa, Bangladesh, Thailand, Malaysia, Sri Lanka, Laos and Vietnam. Despite this diversity, all curries share a few essential elements: a curry paste, seasonings — which can vary from fresh herbs to pungent shrimp paste — and the 'main' ingredient, such as meat, fish, pulses or vegetables. From there, curries can go in many directions. They may be dry, oily, wet, thick or thin. The cooking can involve frying, boiling, steaming or slow, gentle braising. Adjectives such as sour, salty, hot, sweet, creamy, pungent and fragrant may all be applied to a finished dish, more often than not in combination. In fact, if anything unites curries, it is their skill in blending various tastes, textures and aromas to create superb dishes of great depth and balance.

The essential starting place is the curry paste. The paste will infuse the other ingredients with its flavour and fragrance, and its creation is a real part of the pleasure of making a curry. Traditionally, curry pastes are made by hand, the ingredients added one-by-one to a mortar for grinding or to the frying pan for roasting, with the cook observing, smelling and adjusting as necessary. Buying prepared spice mixtures is convenient, but to experience the real thing, have a go at preparing one from scratch.

Of course, the other thing that unites curries is rice. This staple of life is central to the cuisines of India and Southeast Asia, and curries are there to support the rice — not the other way round. Once again, the trick is to seek balance, combining delicately perfumed rice with vegetable dishes, side dishes and curries to match. This book contains some classic raitas, pickles and breads to experiment with and many more wonderful curries that amply demonstrate the delight to be found in this age-old dish.

RICH CURRIES

Creamy, smooth curries are often the best place to start if new to curries. In fact, many of the world's favourite curries belong to this type — the most common examples include butter chicken, Thai Massaman beef curry, Indian lamb kormas and the many kofta, or meatball, recipes that are served resting on a bed of rich, creamy sauce. These curries have coconut milk, ground nuts, yoghurt or cream as their base, sometimes singly but often in combination.

Coconut is perhaps the most versatile of these products. It harmonises flavours, subdues the potency of fiery chillies and balances sour

ingredients such as Thai apple eggplants (aubergines), tart lime juice and salty shrimp paste. The taste of the coconut itself is also important. Fresh coconut cream, in particular, enriches the curry with its own depth of flavour, so that dishes are complex and sumptuous — not merely creamy. Tinned coconut cream does not have the same qualities as fresh coconut but is much easier to obtain. Every part of the coconut tree is used, from thatching for houses to making lotions for the skin and hair from the oil. In India, coconut forms the basis of golden, thick korma-style curries, perfected by the Moguls in the seventeenth century, as well as the yoghurt-based dumpling dishes of Gujarat and the spicy seafood curries of coastal Goa. Thai uses of coconut are just as varied and delicious. Their spicy red curries, the sharp green curries and the panaeng and Massaman curries of the south all have coconut as their starting point.

In contrast to coconut, yoghurt is more often used as a thickener and tenderiser of meat than as a flavouring, producing wonderfully tender, slow-cooked curries of lamb and beef. It is also the key ingredient in soothing Indian raitas, for which many of us have been thankful.

EARTHY CURRIES

The pleasure of many curries begins with the aroma that is released at the start of cooking, as dried spices roast and crackle in the wok or pan. This is especially true of the earthy curries. Spices such as cumin, fennel, coriander seeds, turmeric and curry leaves all bring a warm, rounded, toasty aroma and flavour to curries. For these curries, aroma is of equal importance to flavour and texture.

Taking the time to grind and roast your own spices may seem like a luxury but it is one of the best, and most enjoyable, ways to learn about the different qualities of the spices that go into a curry. Coriander seeds, for example, have a sweet, heady aroma, suggestive of pine and pepper, while warm and bitter cumin is immediately distinctive. Fennel seeds have a subtle anise aroma and warm, sweet, intense flavour that mellows on roasting. Different again are potent cloves, with their sharp and woody flavours contributing to many curry powders, and versatile, pungent turmeric. Hidden within the unassuming dull brown skin of this root is a vibrantly coloured golden interior that, as a ground powder, is used in countless curries to balance and enhance the other flavours.

Earthy curries share a depth of sensuous flavour and aroma that is not always anticipated — which makes cooking and eating them all the more enjoyable.

HOT AND SOUR CURRIES

It has been said that chillies should be treated with respect, and most of us would agree with that. When scanning the ingredient lists of some curries, chillies seem to jump out, regardless of how many other ingredients surround them. Some of us relish the challenge of eating a hot curry; others would prefer to go hungry. But chillies need not — and generally should not — scorch. Rather, they should enhance the overall flavour and fragrance of a dish, with specific chillies being used for their different properties.

Having said that, there are certain curries where no other description besides 'fiery' will do. The jungle curries of Thailand, for example, some of Goa's seafood curries and many Malaysian and Balinese curries fall into this category. Chillies were introduced to Southeast Asia and India in the sixteenth century by traders and spicy dishes can reflect an area's mixed heritage. Goa's notoriously hot vindaloo curry began life as a vinegar and pork dish of the Portuguese, and the Nonya cooking of Malaysia, a mix of indigenous and Chinese cooking, is famous for its hot, tangy and aromatic curries.

The active agent in chillies, capsaicin, is found mostly in the ribs and seeds of chillies. So, seeding a chilli is a fail-safe way of reducing heat levels. Otherwise, use less than the recipe specifies — you can always add more. As a general guide, the smaller the chilli, the hotter it will be.

Chillies are not the only ingredient adding heat to a curry. Mustard seeds and peppercorns can also be extremely potent. But, as with chillies, searing heat is generally not the aim — both of these spices offer a warm, biting flavour and aroma that blend well with other fresh and dried spices and herbs. In particular, hot curries invite the use of sour flavours such as tamarind, tart vinegar and yoghurt and crisp, clean lime juice and lemongrass. The combination of hot and sour is a particularly happy one, with the sour elements adding an extra layer of flavour and fragrance to a hot dish. Sour ingredients also include a number of vegetables — such as bitter melon and Thai apple eggplants (aubergines) — that add textural interest.

AROMATIC CURRIES

Most curries could be described as aromatic, but some specifically favour herbs and spices known primarily for their fragrant qualities. Pepper, chillies and turmeric are all aromatic, but that is not what first comes to mind when thinking about the impact they have on a curry. On the other hand, fresh Thai basil and coriander (cilantro) leaves, cloves and nutmeg all suggest dishes whose aroma — be it sweet, clean, sharp or pungent — immediately invites and seduces.

The frying of the curry paste is a careful exercise in letting your nose tell you when to add the next ingredient.

Thai cooking in particular makes good use of fresh herbs to engage the sense of smell. If Indian cooking excels at combining dried spices, Thai cooking delights in creating curries with layers of flavour and aroma from a wide range of fresh herbs, spices and seasonings. These include local ingredients such as the aniseed-like Thai basil, floral makrut (kaffir lime) leaves and tangy galangal, as well as more familiar ones such as coriander (cilantro), ginger, lemongrass, garlic, spring onions (scallions) and onions. It is sometimes easy to overlook the importance of these reliable ingredients, but few curries could do without the body and flavour they provide, as well as their sharp, clean and sweet aromas.

A Thai green curry is the classic example of this art, blending most of the above with chicken, vegetables or fish in a coconut-based sauce with green chillies for heat. The finished dish — tart, salty and hot — is generously garnished with fresh-tasting, fragrant makrut and Thai basil leaves. Thai curries are renowned for the care taken with the preparation and cooking of ingredients, and the frying of the curry paste is a careful exercise in letting your nose tell you when to add the next ingredient. Learning to recognise the different aromas of herbs and spices is not essential for the occasional curry cook — you'll still produce delicious results — but is certainly something dedicated lovers of curries aspire to.

SWEET CURRIES

Many of the sweet flavours in curries come from introduced ingredients, and it is a testament to the versatility of curries that they can absorb new ingredients and very successfully make them their own. For example, the chilli, native to Central America, could not be more at home in the curries of India and Southeast Asia. But this is true also of perfumed lychees from China, sweet almonds from Persia and juicy tomatoes from South America. Barbecue duck curry with lychees has two of China's most famous ingredients, here seamlessly blended with classic curry spices such as cumin, paprika, turmeric and ground coriander, as well as the ever-present coconut cream, fish sauce and palm sugar. Minted lamb curry transfers the classic combination of fresh, sweet mint and lamb to the world of spicy curries, complementing the fresh herb taste with green chillies, tart lemon juice and sharp cayenne pepper and turmeric.

Sweet ingredients also provide the perfect opportunity for including robust flavours, such as duck and pork, but also seasonings like Indonesia's hot and spicy sambal oelek and fruit such as green bananas. As when blending hot and sour ingredients, sweet and robust flavours are used to complement each other, not compete. An Indian pork, honey and almond curry also contains fresh herbs, citrus zest, spices and yoghurt, all brought magically together through slow, gentle cooking. Snapper with green bananas and mango is another excellent, delicious example of the art of balance that is so central to all curries. The starchy bananas provide texture and act as a thickening agent, the mango contributes a lovely summery sweetness and the fish just absorbs it all, supported by a spicy yellow curry paste and rich coconut cream base.

Chapter 1

RICH CURRY

✦✦✦✦✦✦✦✦✦✦✦✦✦✦✦✦✦✦✦✦✦✦✦✦✦✦✦✦✦✦✦✦✦✦✦✦

Creamy, smooth curries are often the best place to start if new to curries. In fact, many of the world's favourite curries belong to this type — the most common examples include butter chicken, Thai Massaman beef curry, Indian lamb kormas and the many kofta, or meatball, recipes that are served resting on a bed of rich, creamy sauce.

THAI BEEF AND PEANUT CURRY

Like all Thai curries, the key to this dish is balance: it has a sweet, spicy and salty paste combined with the rich smoothness of peanuts and coconut. To roast the peanuts yourself, cook at 180°C (350°F/Gas 4) for 8–10 minutes, or until golden.

CURRY PASTE
8–10 long dried long red chillies
6 red Asian shallots, chopped
6 garlic cloves
1 teaspoon ground coriander
1 tablespoon ground cumin
1 teaspoon ground white pepper
2 lemongrass stems, white part only, sliced
1 tablespoon chopped galangal
6 coriander (cilantro) roots
2 teaspoons shrimp paste
2 tablespoons roasted peanuts
peanut oil, if needed

400 ml (14 fl oz) coconut cream (do not shake the tin)
1 kg (2 lb 4 oz) round or blade steak, thinly sliced
400 ml (14 fl oz) coconut milk
4 makrut (kaffir lime) leaves
90 g (3¼ oz/⅓ cup) crunchy peanut butter
3 tablespoons lime juice
2½ tablespoons fish sauce
2½ tablespoons shaved palm sugar (jaggery)
Thai basil, to serve (optional)
1 tablespoon chopped roasted peanuts, to serve (optional)

Soak the chillies in boiling water for 5 minutes, or until soft. Remove the stem and seeds, then chop. Put the chillies and the remaining curry paste ingredients in a food processor, or in a mortar with a pestle, and process or pound to a smooth paste. Add a little peanut oil if it is too thick.

Put the thick coconut cream from the top of the tin in a saucepan, bring to a rapid simmer over medium heat, stirring occasionally, and cook for 5–10 minutes, or until the mixture splits.

Add 6–8 tablespoons of the curry paste and cook, stirring, for 5–10 minutes, or until fragrant.

Add the beef, the remaining coconut cream, coconut milk, makrut leaves and peanut butter, and cook for 8 minutes, or until the beef just starts to change colour. Reduce the heat and simmer for 1 hour, or until the beef is tender. Stir in the lime juice, fish sauce and palm sugar, and transfer to a serving dish. Garnish with the basil leaves, and extra peanuts, if desired.

SERVES 4–6

Far left: Remove the stem and seeds and chop the softened chillies.

Left: Use a food processor to process the paste ingredients quickly.

Pork Curry with Eggplant

Pork is a favourite meat across much of India and Southeast Asia, but is used in relatively few curries. It is often teamed with other rich flavours, such as coconut. Don't rush this dish, as the slow, gentle cooking ensures the meat is very tender.

CURRY PASTE
4 long red chillies, split lengthways, seeded
1 thick slice galangal, chopped
1 spring onion (scallion), chopped
2 garlic cloves, chopped
2 coriander (cilantro) roots, chopped
1 lemongrass stem, white part only, thinly sliced
1 teaspoon ground white pepper
1/2 teaspoon shrimp paste
1 teaspoon fish sauce
2 tablespoons crunchy peanut butter

600 g (1 lb 5 oz) pork shoulder
1 thick slice ginger
2 tablespoons shaved palm sugar (jaggery)
80 ml (2 1/2 fl oz/1/3 cup) fish sauce
400 ml (14 fl oz) coconut cream (do not shake the tin)
250 g (9 oz) eggplant (aubergine) cut into 2 cm (3/4 in) cubes
225 g (8 oz) tinned bamboo shoots or 140 g (5 oz) drained, sliced
1 large handful Thai basil, chopped

Put the split chillies in a shallow bowl and pour over enough hot water to just cover and rest for 15 minutes, or until softened. Drain, reserving 1 tablespoon of the soaking liquid.

Put the chillies and reserved soaking liquid with the remaining curry paste ingredients, except the peanut butter, in a food processor, or in a mortar with a pestle, and process or pound to a smooth paste. Stir in the peanut butter.

Cut the pork into 1 cm (1/2 in) thick slices. Put in a saucepan and cover with water. Add the ginger slice, 1 tablespoon of the palm sugar and 1 tablespoon of the fish sauce. Bring to the boil over high heat then reduce to a simmer and cook for 20–25 minutes, or until the meat is tender.

Remove from the heat and allow the meat to cool in the liquid stock. Then strain, reserving 250 ml (9 fl oz/1 cup) of the cooking liquid.

Put the thick coconut cream from the top of the tin in a saucepan, bring to a rapid simmer over medium heat, stirring occasionally, and cook for 5–10 minutes, or until the mixture 'splits' (the oil starts to separate). Add the curry paste and remaining palm sugar and fish sauce, and bring to the boil. Reduce to a simmer and cook for about 3 minutes, or until fragrant.

Add the pork, eggplant, sliced bamboo, the reserved pork cooking liquid and the remaining coconut cream. Increase heat and bring to the boil again before reducing to a simmer and cooking for a further 20–25 minutes, or until the eggplant is tender and sauce has thickened slightly. Top with the basil leaves.

SERVES 4

Massaman Vegetable Curry

This curry is sumptuously spiced and seasoned without being fiery or overly rich, and has a lightness of flavour not seen in many meat curries. Similarly, the sauce is thick, neither too wet nor dry, and perfect for scooping up with rice or bread.

MASSAMAN CURRY PASTE
1 tablespoon oil
1 teaspoon coriander seeds
1 teaspoon cumin seeds
8 cloves
1/2 teaspoon fennel seeds
4 cardamom seeds
6 red Asian shallots, chopped
3 garlic cloves, chopped
1 teaspoon lemongrass, finely chopped
1 teaspoon galangal, finely chopped
4 dried long red chillies
1 teaspoon ground nutmeg
1 teaspoon ground white pepper

1 tablespoon oil
250 g (9 oz) baby onions
500 g (1 lb 2 oz) baby new potatoes
300 g (10 1/2 oz) baby carrots, cut into 3 cm (1 1/4 in)
    pieces
225 g (8 oz) button mushrooms (champignons), tinned,
    whole, drained
1 cinnamon stick
1 makrut (kaffir lime) leaf
1 bay leaf
250 ml (9 fl oz/1 cup) coconut cream
1 tablespoon lime juice
3 teaspoons shaved palm sugar (jaggery)
1 tablespoon finely chopped Thai basil, plus extra to
    serve
1 tablespoon crushed roasted peanuts

Heat the oil in a frying pan over low heat, add the coriander seeds, cumin seeds, cloves, fennel seeds and cardamom seeds, and cook for 1–2 minutes, or until fragrant.

Put the spices with the remaining curry paste ingredients in a food processor, or in a mortar with a pestle, and process or pound to a smooth paste. Add a little water if it is too thick.

Heat the oil in a large saucepan, add the curry paste and cook, stirring, over medium heat for

2 minutes, or until fragrant. Add the vegetables, cinnamon stick, makrut leaf, bay leaf and enough water to cover (about 500 ml/17 fl oz/2 cups), and bring to the boil. Reduce the heat and simmer, covered, stirring frequently, for 30–35 minutes, or until the vegetables are cooked.

Stir in the coconut cream and cook, uncovered, for 4 minutes, stirring frequently, until thickened slightly. Stir in the lime juice, palm sugar and chopped basil. Add a little water if the sauce is too dry. Top with the peanuts and basil leaves.

SERVES 4–6

THAI RED DUCK CURRY WITH PINEAPPLE

The art of Thai curries is the way they combine different flavours and textures in the one dish to create a harmonious whole. This dish is a perfect example of that skill; blending sweet, savoury and spicy ingredients with rich coconut milk.

RED CURRY PASTE
15 dried long red chillies
1 tablespoon white peppercorns
2 teaspoons coriander seeds
1 teaspoon cumin seeds
2 teaspoons shrimp paste
5 red Asian shallots, chopped
10 garlic cloves, chopped
2 lemongrass stems, white part only, finely sliced
1 tablespoon chopped galangal
2 tablespoons chopped coriander (cilantro) root
1 teaspoon finely grated makrut (kaffir lime) zest

1 tablespoon peanut oil
8 spring onions (scallions), sliced on the diagonal into
    3 cm (1 1/4 in) lengths
2 garlic cloves, crushed
1 Chinese roast duck, chopped into large pieces
400 ml (14 fl oz) coconut milk
450 g (1 lb) tinned pineapple pieces in syrup, drained
3 makrut (kaffir lime) leaves
3 tablespoons chopped coriander (cilantro) leaves
2 tablespoons chopped mint

Soak the chillies in boiling water for 5 minutes, or until soft. Remove the stem and seeds, then chop. Dry-fry the peppercorns, coriander seeds, cumin seeds, and shrimp paste wrapped in foil in a frying pan over medium–high heat for 2–3 minutes, or until fragrant. Allow to cool. Crush or grind the peppercorns, coriander and cumin to a powder.

Put the chopped chillies, shrimp paste and ground spices with the remaining curry paste ingredients in a food processor, or in a mortar with a pestle, and process or pound to a smooth paste.

Heat a wok until very hot, add the oil and swirl to coat the side. Add the onion, garlic and 2–4 tablespoons red curry paste, and stir-fry for 1 minute, or until fragrant.

Add the roast duck pieces, coconut milk, drained pineapple pieces, makrut leaves, and half the coriander and mint. Bring to the boil, then reduce the heat and simmer for 10 minutes, or until the duck is heated through and the sauce has thickened slightly. Stir in the remaining coriander and mint, and serve.

SERVES 4–6

Split the chillies then scrape away the seeds with a knife.

FISH AND PEANUT CURRY

One of the star ingredients in this dish is crisp fried onion, which can be bought from Asian food stores, or easily prepared at home (see note below). Dried spices and sour tamarind are used to nicely balance the creamy, nutty flavours of this dish.

50 g (1 ¾ oz/⅓ cup) sesame seeds
½ teaspoon cayenne pepper
¼ teaspoon ground turmeric
1 tablespoon desiccated coconut
2 teaspoons ground coriander
½ teaspoon ground cumin
40 g (1 ½ oz/½ cup) crisp fried onion
5 cm (2 in) piece ginger, chopped

2 garlic cloves, chopped
3 tablespoons tamarind purée
1 tablespoon crunchy peanut butter
1 tablespoon roasted peanuts
8 curry leaves, plus extra to serve
1 kg (2 lb 4 oz) firm white fish fillets, cut into skinless
   2 cm (¾ in) cubes
1 tablespoon lemon juice

Put the sesame seeds in a heavy-based frying pan over medium heat and stir until golden. Add the cayenne pepper, turmeric, coconut, ground coriander and ground cumin and stir for a further minute, or until aromatic. Set aside to cool.

Put the fried onions, ginger, garlic, tamarind, 1 teaspoon salt, peanut butter, roasted peanuts, sesame spice mix and 500 ml (17 fl oz/2 cups) hot water in a food processor and process until mixture reaches a smooth, thick consistency.

Put the sauce and curry leaves into a heavy-based frying pan over medium heat and bring to a simmer. Cover and simmer over low heat for 15 minutes, then add the fish in a single layer.

Simmer, covered, for a further 5 minutes, or until the fish is just cooked through. Gently stir through the lemon juice, and season well to taste. Garnish with curry leaves and serve.

Note: To make crisp fried onion at home, very thinly slice 1 onion, then dry on paper towel for 10 minutes. Fill a deep, heavy-based saucepan one-third full of oil and heat to 160°C (315°F), or until a cube of bread dropped into the oil browns in 30 seconds. Fry the onions for up to 1 minute, or until crisp and golden. Drain well, cool and store in an airtight container for up to 2 weeks. Use as a garnish and flavour enhancer for curries, rice and noodle dishes.

SERVES 6

Far left: Stir the sesame seeds over medium heat until lightly golden.

Left: Add the fish in a single layer to the simmering sauce.

Lamb Shank and Yoghurt Curry

This slow-cooked curry produces wonderfully tender meat, while also allowing the subtle aromas and flavours of the spices to blend. It's well worth the wait! The use of yoghurt thickens the sauce and rounds off the dish.

3 tablespoons coriander seeds
2 teaspoons cumin seeds
1 teaspoon cloves
1 teaspoon black peppercorns
1/2 teaspoon cayenne pepper
1 teaspoon ground turmeric
2 tablespoons chopped ginger
6 garlic cloves, chopped

1 small onion, chopped
2 tablespoons ghee or oil
6 lamb shanks
3 cinnamon sticks
2 bay leaves
375 g (13 oz/1 1/2 cups) plain yoghurt
625 ml (21 1/2 fl oz/2 1/2 cups) chicken stock

Preheat the oven to 160°C (315°F/Gas 2–3).

Dry-fry the coriander seeds, cumin seeds, cloves, peppercorns, cayenne pepper and ground turmeric in a frying pan over medium–high heat for 2–3 minutes, or until fragrant. Allow to cool. Using a mortar with a pestle, or a spice grinder, crush or grind to a powder.

Put the ground spices with the ginger, garlic, onion and 3 tablespoons water in a food processor, or in a mortar with a pestle, and process or pound to a smooth paste.

In a large heavy-based frying pan, heat the ghee or oil over medium–high heat and brown the shanks in batches and set aside. Reduce the heat to low. Add the ginger spice paste to the frying pan and

cook for 5–8 minutes. Add the cinnamon, bay leaves and yoghurt to the pan, a spoonful at a time, stirring well so it incorporates smoothly. Add the chicken stock and stir well to combine.

Put the shanks into a large heavy-based ovenproof dish that will fit them in a single layer, then pour the yoghurt sauce over the top of the shanks. Turn the shanks so they are coated with the sauce, and cover with a lid, or foil. Bake in the oven for about 3 hours, or until the lamb is falling from the bone, turning the shanks halfway through cooking. When you remove from the oven, skim any oil that comes to the surface and discard.

Remove the shanks from the sauce onto a serving platter. Season the sauce well to taste, stirring to mix before spooning over the shanks.

SERVES 6

Thai Red Beef Curry with Thai Eggplants

There are many variations on the basic red curry, but all are distinguished by the dark shade of the sauce. The colour comes from the dried long red chillies in the paste. Most red curries are wet and fragrant with fresh makrut (kaffir lime) and Thai basil.

500 g (1 lb 2 oz) round or topside steak
250 ml (9 fl oz / 1 cup) coconut cream (do not shake the tin)
2 tablespoons ready-made red curry paste or see recipe on page 20
2 tablespoons fish sauce

1 tablespoon shaved palm sugar (jaggery)
5 makrut (kaffir lime) leaves, halved
500 ml (17 fl oz / 2 cups) coconut milk
8 Thai apple eggplants (aubergines), halved
1 small handful Thai basil, finely shredded

Cut the meat into 5 cm (2 in) pieces, then cut across the grain at a 45-degree angle into 5 mm (¼ in) thick slices.

Put the thick coconut cream from the top of the tin in a saucepan, bring to a rapid simmer over medium heat, stirring occasionally, and cook for 5–10 minutes, or until the mixture 'splits' (the oil starts to separate). Add the curry paste and simmer, stirring to prevent it sticking to the bottom, for 5 minutes, or until fragrant.

Add the meat and cook, stirring, for 3–5 minutes, or until it changes colour. Add the fish sauce, palm sugar, makrut leaves, coconut milk and remaining coconut cream, and simmer for 1 hour, or until the meat is tender and the sauce slightly thickened.

Add the eggplant and cook for 10 minutes, or until tender. If the sauce is too thick, add a little water. Stir in the basil leaves and serve.

SERVES 4

Lift off the thick coconut cream from the top of the tins.

Rich Chicken Koftas

Kofta might contain meat, fish or vegetables but all are well-combined mixtures, with added herbs and spices. In this dish, the accompanying sauce is rich with coconut, yoghurt, cream and almonds, balanced by the spicy notes of garam masala and turmeric.

KOFTAS

2 tablespoons oil

1 onion, finely chopped

1 garlic clove, crushed

1 teaspoon finely chopped ginger

1 teaspoon ground cumin

1 teaspoon garam masala

1/2 teaspoon ground turmeric

650 g (1 lb 7 oz) chicken thigh fillets, trimmed

2 tablespoons chopped coriander (cilantro) leaves

1 tablespoon ghee or oil

1 onion, roughly chopped

2 garlic cloves, crushed

2 teaspoons garam masala

1/2 teaspoon ground turmeric

170 ml (5 1/2 fl oz/2/3 cup) coconut milk

90 g (3 1/4 oz/1/3 cup) plain yoghurt

125 ml (4 fl oz/1/2 cup) thickened (whipping) cream

35 g (1 1/4 oz/1/3 cup) ground almonds

2 tablespoons chopped coriander (cilantro) leaves

To make the koftas, heat half the oil in a frying pan. Add the onion, garlic, ginger, ground cumin, garam masala and ground turmeric, and cook, stirring, for 4–6 minutes, or until the onion is tender and spices are fragrant. Allow to cool.

Put the chicken fillets in batches in a food processor and process until just chopped.

Put the chicken, onion mixture, coriander and 1/2 teaspoon salt in a bowl, and mix together well. Using wetted hands, measure 1 tablespoon of mixture and shape into a ball. Repeat with the remaining mixture. Heat the remaining oil in a

heavy-based frying pan, add the koftas in batches and cook for 4–5 minutes, or until well browned all over. Remove from the pan and cover. Put the onion in a food processor and process until smooth.

Heat the ghee or oil in a frying pan. Add the onion and garlic, and cook, stirring, for 5 minutes, until the mixture starts to thicken. Add the garam masala and turmeric, and cook for 2 minutes. Add the coconut milk, yoghurt, cream and ground almonds. Bring almost to the boil, then reduce the heat to medium and add the koftas. Cook, stirring occasionally, for 15 minutes, or until the koftas are cooked through. Stir in the coriander and serve.

SERVES 4

Far left: Mix the chicken, onion mixture, coriander and salt together.

Left: Use wetted hands to shape the chicken mixture into balls.

LAMB KORMA

Korma is more than a dish — it is a cooking style. Put simply, it consists of marinated meat or vegetables that are cooked with ghee or oil, then braised with water or stock, yoghurt or cream (or sometimes all of these).

1 kg (2 lb 4 oz) lamb leg meat
1 onion, chopped, plus 1 onion, sliced
2 teaspoons grated ginger
4 garlic cloves
2 teaspoons ground coriander
2 teaspoons ground cumin
1 teaspoon cardamom seeds
1/4 teaspoon cloves
1/4 teaspoon ground cinnamon
3 long green chillies, seeded, chopped
2 tablespoons ghee or oil

2 1/2 tablespoons tomato paste (concentrated purée)
125 g (4 1/2 oz/1/2 cup) plain yoghurt
125 ml (4 fl oz/1/2 cup) coconut cream
50 g (1 3/4 oz/1/2 cup) ground almonds
toasted slivered almonds, to serve

Trim any excess fat or sinew from the lamb, cut into 3 cm (1 1/4 in) cubes and put in a large bowl.

Put the chopped onion, ginger, garlic, coriander, cumin, cardamom seeds, cloves, cinnamon, chilli and 1/2 teaspoon salt in a food processor, or in a mortar with a pestle, and process or pound to a smooth paste. Add the spice paste to the lamb and mix well to coat. Leave to marinate for 1 hour.

Heat the ghee or oil in a large saucepan, add the sliced onion and cook, stirring, over low heat for

7 minutes, or until the onion is soft. Increase the heat to medium–high and add the lamb mixture and cook, stirring constantly, for 8–10 minutes, or until the lamb changes colour.

Stir in the tomato paste, yoghurt, coconut cream and ground almonds. Reduce the heat and simmer, covered, stirring occasionally, for about 1 hour, or until the meat is very tender. Add a little water if the mixture becomes too dry. Season well with salt and pepper, and serve garnished with the slivered almonds.

SERVES 4

Far left: Add the spice paste to the lamb and leave to marinate.

Left: Add the lamb mixture to the pan and cook until it changes colour.

Scallops and Prawns Chu Chee

Chu Chee curry paste is the traditional Thai flavour base for seafood. It is similar to a red curry paste, in that dried red chillies dominate, but the proportion of aromatics such as galangal, makrut (kaffir lime) leaves and coriander (cilantro) are greater.

CHU CHEE CURRY PASTE
10 long red chillies, dried
1 teaspoon coriander seeds
1 tablespoon shrimp paste
1 tablespoon white peppercorns
10 makrut (kaffir lime) leaves, finely shredded
10 red Asian shallots, chopped
2 teaspoons finely grated makrut (kaffir lime) zest
1 tablespoon chopped coriander (cilantro) stem and root, chopped
1 stem lemongrass, white part only, finely chopped
3 tablespoons chopped galangal
1 tablespoon chopped krachai, optional (see note)
6 garlic cloves, crushed

540 ml (18½ fl oz) tinned coconut cream (do not shake the tins)
500 g (1 lb 2 oz) scallops with roe removed
500 g (1 lb 2 oz) raw king prawns (shrimp), peeled, deveined, tails intact
2–3 tablespoons fish sauce
2–3 tablespoons palm sugar (jaggery)
8 makrut (kaffir lime) leaves, finely shredded
2 red chillies, thinly sliced
1 large handful Thai basil

Soak the chillies in boiling water for 5 minutes, or until soft. Remove the stem and seeds, then chop. Dry-fry the coriander seeds, shrimp paste wrapped in foil, and peppercorns in a frying pan over medium–high heat for 2–3 minutes, or until fragrant. Allow to cool. Using a mortar with a pestle, or a spice grinder, crush or grind the coriander and peppercorns to a powder.

Put the chopped chillies, shrimp paste and ground coriander and peppercorns with the remaining curry paste ingredients in a food processor, or in a mortar with a pestle, and process or pound to a smooth paste.

Put the thick coconut cream from the top of the tins in a saucepan, bring to a rapid simmer over medium heat, stirring occasionally, and cook for 5–10 minutes, or until the mixture 'splits' (the oil starts to separate). Stir in 3 tablespoons of the curry paste, reduce the heat and simmer for 10 minutes, or until fragrant.

Stir in the remaining coconut cream, scallops and prawns, and cook for 5 minutes, or until tender. Add the fish sauce, palm sugar, makrut leaves and chilli, and cook for 1 minute. Stir in half the Thai basil and garnish with the remaining leaves.

Note: Krachai (bottled lesser galangal) is available from Asian food stores. It can be omitted from the paste if unavailable.

SERVES 4

BUTTER CHICKEN

For many westerners, this famous dish is their first experience of Indian food. Based on tandoori chicken, but without the tandoor, it is a rich blend of aromatic spices, butter or ghee, yoghurt and tomato paste.

2 tablespoons peanut oil
1 kg (2 lb 4 oz), quartered chicken thigh fillets
100 g (3½ oz) butter or ghee
3 teaspoons garam masala
2 teaspoons sweet paprika
1 tablespoon ground coriander
1 tablespoon finely chopped ginger
3 teaspoons ground cumin
2 garlic cloves, crushed

¼ teaspoon chilli powder
1 cinnamon stick
5 cardamom pods, bruised
2½ tablespoons tomato paste (concentrated purée)
1 tablespoon sugar
90 g (3¼ oz/⅓ cup) plain yoghurt
185 ml (6 fl oz/¾ cup) cream (whipping)
1 tablespoon lemon juice

Heat a frying pan or wok until very hot, add 1 tablespoon oil and swirl to coat. Add half the chicken thigh fillets and stir-fry for 4 minutes, or until browned. Remove from the pan. Add extra oil, as needed, and cook the remaining chicken, then remove.

Reduce the heat, add the butter to the pan or wok and melt. Add the garam masala, sweet paprika, coriander, ginger, cumin, garlic, chilli powder,

cinnamon stick and cardamom pods, and stir-fry for 1 minute, or until fragrant. Return the chicken to the pan and mix in the spices so it is well coated.

Add the tomato paste and sugar, and simmer, stirring, for 15 minutes, or until the chicken is tender and the sauce has thickened. Add the yoghurt, cream and lemon juice and simmer for 5 minutes, or until the sauce has thickened slightly.

SERVES 4-6

Far left: Stir-fry the spices in a frying pan or wok until fragrant.

Left: Stir in the tomato paste and sugar and simmer.

Massaman Beef Curry

This rich, creamy curry is a classic among Thai curries. Its origins are unclear but today it is associated with the southern areas of Thailand. Complex, with sweet and sour spices, it is unusual in that it incorporates a starchy ingredient such as potatoes.

1 tablespoon tamarind pulp

2 tablespoons oil

750 g (1 lb 10 oz) lean stewing beef, cubed

500 ml (17 fl oz/2 cups) coconut milk

4 cardamom pods, bruised

500 ml (17 fl oz/2 cups) tinned coconut cream (do not shake the tins)

2–3 tablespoons ready-made Massaman curry paste or see recipe on page 19

8 baby onions

8 large baby potatoes, cut in half

2 tablespoons fish sauce

2 tablespoons shaved palm sugar (jaggery)

70 g (2½ oz/½ cup) unsalted roasted ground peanuts

coriander (cilantro) leaves, to serve

Put the tamarind pulp and 125 ml (4 fl oz/½ cup) boiling water in a bowl and set aside to cool. When cool, mash the pulp to dissolve in the water, then strain and reserve the liquid. Discard the pulp.

Heat the oil in a wok or a large saucepan and cook the beef in batches over high heat for 5 minutes, or until browned. Reduce the heat and add the coconut milk and cardamom, and simmer for 1 hour, or until the beef is tender. Remove the beef, strain and reserve the beef and cooking liquid.

Put the thick coconut cream from the top of the tins in a saucepan, bring to a rapid simmer over medium heat, stirring occasionally, and cook for 5–10 minutes, or until the mixture 'splits' (the oil starts to separate). Add the curry paste and cook for 5 minutes, or until it becomes aromatic.

Add the onions, potatoes, fish sauce, palm sugar, peanuts, beef, reserved cooking liquid and tamarind liquid, and simmer for 25–30 minutes. Garnish with fresh coriander leaves.

SERVES 4

Right: Pour boiling water onto the tamarind pulp to soften it.

Far right: Mash the pulp together with the water until as smooth as possible.

THAI YELLOW VEGETABLE CURRY

Yellow curries are from Thailand's southern areas and are characterised by their use of spices such as coriander, cumin and turmeric in the paste — the turmeric providing the lovely golden colouring. They are usually of medium strength and delicately spiced.

YELLOW CURRY PASTE
8 green chillies
5 red Asian shallots, chopped
2 garlic cloves, crushed
1 tablespoon finely chopped coriander (cilantro) stem
    and root
1 lemongrass stem, white part only, finely chopped
2 tablespoons finely chopped galangal
1 teaspoon ground coriander
1 teaspoon ground cumin
1/2 teaspoon ground turmeric
1/2 teaspoon black peppercorns
1 tablespoon lime juice

3 tablespoons oil
1 onion finely chopped
200 g (7 oz) all-purpose potatoes, diced
200 g (7 oz) zucchini (courgette), diced
150 g (5 1/2 oz) red capsicum (pepper), diced
100 g (3 1/2 oz) halved beans, trimmed
50 g (1 3/4 oz) bamboo shoots, sliced
250 ml (9 fl oz/1 cup) vegetable stock
400 ml (14 fl oz) coconut cream
Thai basil, to serve

Put all the curry paste ingredients in a food processor, or in a mortar with a pestle, and process or pound to a smooth paste.

Heat the oil in a large saucepan, add the onion and cook over medium heat for 4–5 minutes, or until softened and just turning golden. Add 2 tablespoons of the made yellow curry paste and cook, stirring, for 2 minutes, or until fragrant.

Add all the vegetables and cook, stirring, over high heat for 2 minutes. Pour in the vegetable stock, reduce the heat to medium and cook, covered, for 15–20 minutes, or until the vegetables are tender. Cook, uncovered, over high heat for 5–10 minutes, or until the sauce has reduced slightly.

Stir in the coconut cream and season with salt to taste. Bring to the boil, stirring frequently, then reduce the heat and simmer for 5 minutes. Garnish with the Thai basil leaves.

SERVES 6

Chapter 2

EARTHY CURRY

The pleasure of many curries begins with the aroma that is released as
dried spices roast and crackle in the wok or pan. This is especially true of
the earthy curries. Spices such as cumin, fennel, coriander seeds, turmeric
and curry leaves bring a warm, rounded, toasty aroma and flavour to
these curries where aroma is of equal importance to flavour and texture.

Chicken and Thai Apple Eggplant Curry

This savoury curry has lots of flavour and is well balanced — not too hot, sweet or sour. Thai apple eggplants (aubergine) can be an acquired taste. When fresh, they are crisp and clean and almost sweet tasting, but when old and musty, become quite bitter.

CURRY PASTE
1 teaspoon white peppercorns
2 tablespoons dried shrimp
1 teaspoon shrimp paste
2 tablespoons chopped coriander (cilantro) root
3 lemongrass stems, white part only, thinly sliced
3 garlic cloves
1 tablespoon finely chopped ginger
1 red chilli, chopped
4 makrut (kaffir lime) leaves
3 tablespoons fish sauce
3 tablespoons lime juice
1 teaspoon ground turmeric

500 g (1 lb 2 oz) chicken thigh fillets
250 g (9 oz) Thai apple eggplant (aubergine)
400 ml (14 fl oz) coconut cream (do not shake the tin)
2 tablespoons shaved palm sugar (jaggery)
1 red capsicum (pepper), sliced
230 g (8½ oz) tinned water chestnuts, sliced, drained
1 tablespoon chopped coriander (cilantro) leaves
1 tablespoon chopped Thai basil

Dry-fry the peppercorns, dried shrimp and the shrimp paste wrapped in some foil in a frying pan over medium–high heat for 2–3 minutes, or until fragrant. Allow to cool. Using a mortar with a pestle, or a spice grinder, crush or grind the peppercorns to a powder. Process the dried shrimp in a food processor until it becomes very finely shredded — forming a 'floss'.

Put the crushed peppercorns, shredded dried shrimp and the shrimp paste with the remaining curry paste ingredients in a food processor, or in a mortar with a pestle, and process or pound to a smooth paste.

Cut the chicken thigh fillets into 2.5 cm (1 in) cubes. Cut the eggplant into pieces of a similar size.

Put the thick coconut cream from the top of the tin in a saucepan, bring to a rapid simmer over medium heat, stirring occasionally, and cook for 5–10 minutes, or until the mixture 'splits' (the oil starts to separate). Add the curry paste and stir for 5–6 minutes, or until fragrant. Add the palm sugar and stir until dissolved.

Add the chicken, eggplant, capsicum, half the remaining coconut cream and the water chestnuts. Bring to the boil, cover and reduce to a simmer and cook for 15 minutes, or until the chicken is cooked and eggplant soft. Stir in the remaining coconut cream, coriander and basil.

Note: Thai apple eggplants are available at Asian food stores over summer and into early autumn.

SERVES 4

Sri Lankan Pepper Beef Curry

Sri Lankan cuisine has been influenced by the Indians, Malays, Portuguese, Dutch and British. Its curries are mostly coconut based, and strong with spices. Many are cooked for hours until the thick, flavoursome sauce clings to the tender main ingredient.

1 tablespoon coriander seeds
2 teaspoons cumin seeds
1 teaspoon fennel seeds
1 tablespoon black peppercorns
3 tablespoons oil
1 kg (2 lb 4 oz) beef chuck, diced
2 onions, finely diced
2 garlic cloves, crushed

3 teaspoons finely grated ginger
1 red chilli seeded, finely chopped
8 curry leaves
1 lemongrass stem, white part only, finely chopped
2 tablespoons lemon juice
250 ml (9 fl oz/1 cup) coconut milk
250 ml (9 fl oz/1 cup) beef stock

Dry-fry the coriander seeds, cumin seeds, fennel seeds, and black peppercorns in a frying pan over medium–high heat for 2–3 minutes, or until fragrant. Allow to cool. Using a mortar with a pestle, or a spice grinder, crush or grind to a powder.

In a heavy-based saucepan, heat the oil over high heat, brown the beef in batches, and set aside. Reduce heat to medium, add the onion, garlic, ginger, chilli, curry leaves, and lemongrass, and cook for 5–6 minutes, or until softened. Add the ground spices and cook for a further 3 minutes.

Put the beef back into the pan, and stir well to coat in the spices. Add the lemon juice, coconut milk and beef stock and bring to the boil. Reduce heat to low, cover and cook for 2½ hours, or until the beef is very tender and the sauce is reduced. While cooking, skim any oil that comes to the surface and discard.

SERVES 6

Right: Stir the spices constantly to release the aroma.

Far right: Brown the beef in batches to ensure you don't crowd the pan.

BURMESE CHICKEN CURRY

Not surprisingly for a country bordered by five other countries, the cuisine of Myanmar (Burma) shows various outside influences — in particular Thai, Indian and Chinese. Burmese curries are full of aromatic flavours but not as spicy as Indian ones.

1 tablespoon medium-spiced Indian curry powder

1 teaspoon garam masala

½ teaspoon cayenne pepper

2 teaspoons sweet paprika

1.6 kg (3 lb 8 oz) whole chicken cut into 8 pieces or 1.6 kg (3 lb 8 oz) mixed chicken pieces

2 onions, chopped

3 garlic cloves, crushed

2 teaspoons grated ginger

2 tomatoes, chopped

2 teaspoons tomato paste (concentrated purée)

1 lemongrass stem, white part only, thinly sliced

3 tablespoons oil

500 ml (17 fl oz/2 cups) chicken stock

½ teaspoon sugar

1 tablespoon fish sauce

Mix the curry powder, garam masala, cayenne pepper and paprika in a bowl. Rub this spice mix all over the chicken pieces and set aside.

Put the onions, garlic, ginger, tomatoes, tomato paste and lemongrass in a food processor, or in a mortar with a pestle, and process or pound to a smooth paste.

In a large heavy-based frying pan (that will fit the chicken pieces in a single layer), heat the oil over medium heat, add the chicken and brown all over, then remove from the pan. In the same frying pan, add the onion paste and cook over low heat for 5–8 minutes stirring constantly. Put the chicken back into the pan, and turn to coat in the paste.

Add the chicken stock and sugar and bring to a simmer. Reduce heat to low, cover and cook for 1¼ hours, or until the chicken is very tender. While cooking, skim any oil that comes to the surface and discard. Stir in the fish sauce and serve.

SERVES 6

Far left: Rub the spice mixture well into the chicken pieces.

Left: Process or pound the paste ingredients until smooth.

Beef Rendang

In this festive dish of Indonesia and Malaysia, beef is cooked until tender and coated in a rich, thick sauce, permeated with the warm, complex aroma and flavour of spices and seasonings. It is easy to make, with everything going into the one pot.

1.5 kg (3 lb 5 oz) beef chuck
2 onions, roughly chopped
2 garlic cloves, crushed
400 ml (14 fl oz) coconut milk
2 teaspoons ground coriander
½ teaspoon ground fennel

2 teaspoons ground cumin
¼ teaspoon ground cloves
4–6 red chillies, chopped
1 tablespoon lemon juice
1 lemongrass stem, white part only, cut lengthways
2 teaspoons shaved palm sugar (jaggery)

Trim the meat of any excess fat or sinew and cut into 3 cm (1¼ in) cubes. Put the onion and garlic in a food processor, or in a mortar with a pestle, and process or pound to a smooth paste.

Put the coconut milk in a large saucepan and bring to the boil, then reduce the heat to medium and cook, stirring occasionally, for 15 minutes, or until the milk has reduced by half and the oil has separated. Do not allow the milk to brown.

Add the coriander, fennel, cumin and cloves to the pan, and stir for 1 minute. Add the meat and cook for 2 minutes, or until it changes colour. Add the onion mixture, chilli, lemon juice, lemongrass and sugar. Cook, covered, over medium heat for 2 hours, or until the liquid has reduced and the mixture has thickened. Stir frequently to prevent it sticking to the bottom of the pan.

Uncover and continue cooking until the oil from the coconut milk begins to emerge again, letting the curry develop colour and flavour. Be careful that it does not burn. The curry is cooked when it is brown and dry.

SERVES 6

Far left: Simmer the coconut milk until the oil 'splits' or separates.

Left: Add the spices to the coconut milk and cook until fragrant.

Lamb Dhansak

This rich curry comes from the parsees of west India, who emigrated there from Iran in the seventh century. It is striking for the number of different lentils used, as well as vegetables such as English spinach and pumpkin, various spices and tender lamb.

100 g (3½ oz/¾ cup) yellow lentils

2 teaspoons dried yellow mung beans

2 tablespoons dried chickpeas

3 tablespoons red lentils

1 unpeeled eggplant (aubergine)

150 g (5½ oz) unpeeled pumpkin (winter squash)

2 tablespoons ghee or oil

1 onion, finely chopped

3 garlic cloves, crushed

1 tablespoon grated ginger

1 kg (2 lb 4 oz) boneless leg or shoulder of lamb, cut into 3 cm (1¼ in) cubes

1 cinnamon stick

5 cardamom pods, bruised

3 cloves

1 tablespoon ground coriander

1 teaspoon ground turmeric

1 teaspoon chilli powder, or to taste

150 g (5½ oz) amaranth or English spinach leaves, cut into 5 cm (2 in) lengths

2 tomatoes, halved

2 long green chillies, seeded, split lengthways

3 tablespoons lime juice

Soak the yellow lentils, yellow mung beans and chickpeas in water for about 2 hours, then drain well.

Put all four types of pulse in a saucepan, add 1 litre (35 fl oz/4 cups) water, cover and bring to the boil. Uncover and simmer for 15 minutes, skimming off any scum that forms on the surface, and stirring occasionally to make sure all the pulses are cooking at the same rate and are soft. Drain the pulses and lightly mash to a similar texture.

Cook the eggplant and pumpkin in boiling water for 10–15 minutes, or until soft. Scoop out the pumpkin flesh and cut it into pieces. Peel the eggplant carefully (it may be very pulpy) and cut the flesh into small pieces.

Heat the ghee or oil in a casserole dish or karahi (see note below) and fry the onion, garlic and ginger for 5 minutes, or until lightly brown and softened. Add the lamb and brown for 10 minutes, or until aromatic. Add the cinnamon, cardamom pods, cloves, coriander, turmeric and chilli powder and fry for 5 minutes to allow the flavours to develop. Add 170 ml (5½ fl oz/⅔ cup) water, cover and simmer for 40 minutes, or until the lamb is tender.

Add the mashed lentils and all the cooked and raw vegetables to the pan. Add the lime juice and simmer for 15 minutes (if the sauce is too thick, add a little water). Stir well, then check the seasoning. The dhansak should be flavoursome, aromatic, tart and spicy.

Note: A karahi is a deep, wok-shaped cooking dish used in Indian and Balti cooking. It lends itself perfectly to one-pot meals and can be taken straight from the stove to the table for serving.

SERVES 6

Spicy Prawns

Turmeric is at the heart of so many curries. It imparts not just colour, but also a subtle aroma and earthy, slightly bitter flavour. Using ground turmeric is easy and convenient but buy some fresh turmeric root if you see it — it looks similar to old ginger.

1 kg (2 lb 4 oz) raw prawns (shrimp), peeled, deveined,
  tails intact (reserve shells and heads)
1 teaspoon ground turmeric
3 tablespoons oil
2 onions, finely chopped
4–6 garlic cloves, crushed
1–2 green chillies, seeded, chopped

2 teaspoons ground cumin
2 teaspoons ground coriander
1 teaspoon paprika
90 g (3½ oz/⅓ cup) plain yoghurt
80 ml (2½ fl oz/⅓ cup) thickened (whipping) cream
1 large handful coriander (cilantro) leaves, chopped

Bring 1 litre (35 fl oz/4 cups) water to the boil in a saucepan. Add the reserved prawn shells and heads, reduce the heat and simmer for 2 minutes. Skim any scum that forms on the surface during cooking. Strain, discard the shells and heads and return the liquid to the pan. You will need about 750 ml (26 fl oz/3 cups) liquid (make up with water if necessary). Add the turmeric and peeled prawns, and cook for 1 minute, or until the prawns just turn pink, then remove the prawns. Reserve the stock.

Heat the oil in a large saucepan. Add the onion and cook over a medium heat, stirring, for 8 minutes, or until lightly golden brown. Add the garlic and chilli, and cook for 1–2 minutes, then add the cumin, coriander and paprika, and cook, stirring, for 1–2 minutes, or until fragrant.

Gradually add the reserved stock, bring to the boil and cook, stirring occasionally, for 30–35 minutes, or until the mixture has reduced by half and thickened. Remove from the heat and stir in the yoghurt. Add the prawns and stir over low heat for 2–3 minutes, or until the prawns are warmed through. Do not boil. Stir in the cream and coriander leaves. Cover and leave to stand for 15 minutes to allow the flavours to infuse. Reheat gently and serve.

SERVES 4-6

Far left: Simmer the prawn shells and heads, skimming the surface.

Left: Poach the prawns in the stock until just pink and curled.

FISH IN YOGHURT CURRY

The creamy texture of this dish belies the depth of flavour it has from the cumin, coriander and turmeric. Thick yoghurt is an excellent way to protect the fish during cooking and also absorbs some of the sting from the chillies. Use a thick, set yoghurt.

1 kg (2 lb 4 oz) skinless, firm white fish fillets
3 tablespoons oil
1 onion, chopped
2 tablespoons finely chopped ginger
6 garlic cloves, crushed
1 teaspoon ground cumin

2 teaspoons ground coriander
1/4 teaspoon ground turmeric
1 teaspoon garam masala
185 g (6 1/2 oz/3/4 cup) Greek-style yoghurt
4 long green chillies, seeded, finely chopped
coriander (cilantro) leaves, to serve

Cut each fish fillet into four pieces and thoroughly pat them dry. Heat the oil in a heavy-based frying pan over low heat and fry the onion until softened and lightly browned. Add the ginger, garlic and spices and stir for 2 minutes. Add the yoghurt and green chilli and bring to the boil, then cover and simmer for 10 minutes.

Slide in the pieces of fish and continue to simmer for 10–12 minutes, or until the fish flakes easily and is cooked through. Don't overcook or the fish will give off liquid and the sauce will split.

Garnish with coriander leaves and serve immediately. If you let the dish sit, the fish may give off liquid and make the sauce more runny.

SERVES 4

Beef and Mustard Seed Curry

This comforting curry looks after itself once the initial frying of the spices is done. Stay close while cooking the spices to ensure that they do not burn. The mustard seeds, in particular, give this dish a distinctive nutty taste.

3 tablespoons oil
2 tablespoons brown mustard seeds
4 dried red chillies
1 tablespoon yellow split peas
200 g (7 oz) French shallots finely, sliced
8 garlic cloves, crushed

1 tablespoon finely grated ginger
15 curry leaves
½ teaspoon ground turmeric
420 g (15 oz) tinned chopped tomatoes
1 kg (2 lb 4 oz) beef chuck, diced
435 ml (15½ fl oz/1¾ cups) beef stock

Put the oil in a heavy-based saucepan over medium heat, add the mustard seeds, chillies and split peas. As soon as the mustard seeds start to pop, add the shallots, garlic, ginger, curry leaves and turmeric. Cook for 5 minutes, then add the tomatoes, beef and stock.

Bring to the boil then reduce to a simmer, cover and cook for 2 hours, or until the beef is very tender and the sauce reduced. While cooking, skim any oil that comes to the surface and discard.

SERVES 6

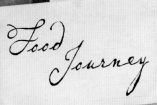

BREADS

Roti is the generic name for bread or bread-like accompaniments. There is a great variety and they are baked, grilled (broiled), roasted or fried. There is no rule regarding which type of roti goes with which dish but it's a rare curry that does not happily lend itself to being scooped up with some bread.

Roti are popular all over Asia and especially in the northern and central areas of India where wheat and grains are staples, rather than rice. Although it is a common assumption that rice is part of every meal, there are actually vast areas of Asia that don't have the right climate or terrain for rice growing. Therefore, these areas produce different grains and have a large repertoire of roti which commonly accompany meals.

In northern and central India, roti are eaten with every meal instead of rice. Throughout the rest of India, roti as well as rice are eaten with main meals every day. Roti function both as part of the meal and as a handy eating tool because they are used to scoop up the more liquid dishes including dal, or to pick up pieces of meat. Roti are also utilized as wrappers for grilled (broiled) meats, or as edible plates, with the accompaniments piled on top, at roadside stalls.

Roti made from wheat are generally cooked in one of four ways: on a tava (a flat, convex or concave griddle) without the use of fat, or on a tava using a little ghee or oil, or deep-fried in a karhai, or baked in a tandoor or oven. Each of the first three methods gives a different result using essentially the same unleavened dough. Sometimes, as for parathas, the dough is layered with ghee to give a flaky texture. At other times, it may be covered as it cooks to create a softer texture. Baked roti are made from leavened dough.

Unleavened roti cooked on a tava include chapatis, rumali, and phulkas (a type of chapati which is made to puff up by briefly cooking it on hot coals) as well as roti flavoured with spinach. Those cooked with fat are parathas. The most common deep-fried bread is the puri, which ranges from the tiny mouthfuls (gol goppas) used to make chaat, such as pani puri, to those bigger ones eaten with meals. Poppadoms are also a deep-fried accompaniment, though unlike the softer roti they are made from a dough of ground pulses and form a very thin, crisp disc with a bubbled surface.

Leavened breads rely on the intense, all-round heat of an oven or tandoor to make them rise and cook in minutes. The breads are stuck to the oven wall for a few minutes. They include naan, kulcha and sheermal. Baked breads are common to areas such as the Punjab, Hyderabad and Kashmir where ovens or tandoors (often communal) are commonly used. In other areas, baked breads are produced by restaurants as domestic kitchens do not have suitable ovens.

Other bread-like accompaniments include pancakes and cakes made of rice and gram, either steamed or cooked on griddles, such as idlis, appams and dosas.

Onion Bhaji Curry

These bhajis get their distinctive taste and colour from nutty-tasting, yellow besan flour and turmeric. They also contain asafoetida, a dried resin whose pungent aroma has earned it the name 'devil's dung'.

2 tablespoons oil
1 teaspoon grated ginger
2 garlic cloves, crushed
425 g (15 oz) tinned crushed tomatoes
¼ teaspoon ground turmeric
½ teaspoon chilli powder
1½ teaspoons ground cumin
1 teaspoon ground coriander
1½ tablespoons garam masala
250 ml (9 fl oz/1 cup) thickened (whipping) cream
chopped coriander (cilantro) leaves, to serve

BHAJIS
125 g (4½ oz/1¼ cups) besan (chickpea flour)
¼ teaspoon ground turmeric
½ teaspoon chilli powder
¼ teaspoon asafoetida
1 onion, thinly sliced
oil for deep-frying

Heat the oil in a frying pan, add the ginger and garlic, and cook for 2 minutes, or until fragrant. Add the tomato, turmeric, chilli powder, cumin, coriander and 250 ml (9 fl oz/1 cup) water. Bring to the boil, then reduce the heat and simmer for 5 minutes, or until thickened slightly. Add the garam masala, stir in the cream and simmer for 1–2 minutes. Remove from heat.

To make the bhajis, combine the besan, turmeric, chilli powder and asafoetida with 125 ml (4 fl oz/½ cup) water, and salt to taste. Whisk to make a smooth batter, then stir in the onion.

Fill a deep heavy-based saucepan one-third full of oil and heat to 160°C (315°F), or until a cube of bread dropped into the oil browns in 30 seconds. Add spoonfuls of the onion mixture in batches and cook for 1–2 minutes, or until golden brown all over, then drain on paper towel. Pour the sauce over the bhajis and garnish with the coriander leaves.

SERVES 4

Far left: Coat the sliced onion well in the smooth besan batter.

Left: Deep-fry spoonfuls of the bhaji mixture until crisp and golden.

MALAYSIAN CHICKEN CURRY

Malaysian cuisine is an exciting mix of outside influences with its own, often highly regional, distinctive characteristics. Curries often draw on the spices of India and the seasonings of Thai curries, blending them with coconut milk, chillies and candlenuts.

3 teaspoons dried shrimp
80 ml (2½ fl oz/⅓ cup) oil
6–8 red chillies, seeded, finely chopped
4 garlic cloves, crushed
3 lemongrass stems, white part only, finely chopped
2 teaspoons ground turmeric

10 candlenuts
2 large onions, chopped
250 ml (9 fl oz/1 cup) coconut milk
1.5 kg (3 lb 5 oz) whole chicken, cut into 8 pieces
125 ml (4 fl oz/½ cup) coconut cream
2 tablespoons lime juice

Put the shrimp in a frying pan and dry-fry over low heat, shaking the pan regularly, for 3 minutes, or until the shrimp are dark orange and are giving off a strong aroma. Allow to cool.

Put the shrimp, half the oil, chilli, garlic, lemongrass, turmeric and candlenuts in a food processor, or in a mortar with a pestle, and process or pound to a smooth paste.

Heat the remaining oil in a wok or frying pan, add the onion and ¼ teaspoon salt, and cook, stirring regularly, over low–medium heat for 8 minutes, or until golden. Add the spice paste and stir for

5 minutes. If the mixture begins to stick to the bottom of the pan, add 2 tablespoons coconut milk. It is important to cook the mixture thoroughly as this develops the flavours.

Add the chicken to the wok or pan and cook, stirring, for 5 minutes, or until it begins to brown. Stir in the remaining coconut milk and 250 ml (9 fl oz/1 cup) water, and bring to the boil. Reduce the heat and simmer for 50 minutes, or until the chicken is cooked and the sauce has thickened slightly. Add the coconut cream and bring the mixture back to the boil, stirring constantly. Add the lime juice and serve immediately.

SERVES 4-6

Far left: Dry-fry the shrimp until dark orange and aromatic.

Left: If using a food processor, scrape down the sides of the bowl.

Spinach Koftas in Yoghurt Sauce

Gujarati dishes such as this are unique in India in that they are nearly always vegetarian. Curries are typically mild and rely on fresh vegetables, yoghurt, and accompanying pickles and chutneys for extra spice.

YOGHURT SAUCE

375 g (13 oz/1 1/2 cups) plain yoghurt
35 g (1 1/4 oz/1/3 cup) besan (chickpea flour)
1 tablespoon oil
2 teaspoons black mustard seeds
1 teaspoon fenugreek seeds
6 curry leaves
1 large onion, finely chopped
3 garlic cloves, crushed
1 teaspoon ground turmeric
1/2 teaspoon chilli powder

KOFTAS

450 g (1 lb/1 bunch) English spinach, leaves picked off
    the stems
170 g (6 oz/1 1/2 cups) besan (chickpea flour)
1 red onion, finely chopped
1 ripe tomato, finely diced
2 garlic cloves, crushed
1 teaspoon ground cumin
2 tablespoons chopped coriander (cilantro) leaves
oil for deep-frying
coriander (cilantro) leaves, to serve

To make the yoghurt sauce whisk the yoghurt, besan and 750 ml (26 fl oz/3 cups) water in a bowl, to a smooth paste. Heat the oil in a heavy-based saucepan or deep frying pan over low heat.

Add the mustard and fenugreek seeds and the curry leaves, cover and allow the seeds to pop for 1 minute. Add the onion and cook for 5 minutes, or until soft and starting to brown.

Add the garlic and stir for 1 minute, or until soft. Add the turmeric and chilli powder and stir for 30 seconds. Add the yoghurt mixture, bring to the boil and simmer over low heat for 10 minutes.

To make the spinach koftas, blanch the spinach in boiling water for 1 minute and refresh in cold water. Drain, squeeze out any extra water by putting the spinach in a colander and pressing it against the sides with a spoon. Finely chop the spinach. Combine with the remaining kofta ingredients and up to 3 tablespoons water, a little at a time, adding enough to make the mixture soft but not sloppy. If it becomes too sloppy, add more besan. Shape the mixture into balls by rolling it in dampened hands, using about 1 tablespoon of mixture for each. This should make 12 koftas.

Fill a heavy-based saucepan one-third full with oil and heat to 180°C (350°F), or until a cube of bread browns in 15 seconds. Lower the koftas into the oil in batches and fry until golden and crisp. Don't overcrowd the pan. Remove the koftas as they cook, shake off any excess oil and add them to the yoghurt sauce. Gently reheat the yoghurt sauce, garnish with coriander leaves and serve.

SERVES 4

Dal

In India, dal refers to both the dried pulse and the finished dish. To bolster the simple flavour of the lentils, spices such as cumin and asafoetida are fried in ghee, releasing their earthy aromas.

200 g (7 oz/³/₄ cup) red lentils
3 thick slices ginger
½ teaspoon ground turmeric
1 tablespoon ghee or oil
2 garlic cloves, crushed
1 onion, finely chopped

½ teaspoon yellow mustard seeds
pinch asafoetida, optional
1 teaspoon cumin seeds
1 teaspoon ground coriander
2 green chillies, halved lengthways
2 tablespoons lemon juice

Put the lentils and 750 ml (26 fl oz/3 cups) water in a saucepan, and bring to the boil. Reduce the heat, add the ginger and turmeric, and simmer, covered, for 20 minutes, or until the lentils are tender. Stir occasionally to prevent the lentils sticking to the pan. Remove the ginger and season the lentil mixture with salt.

Heat the ghee or oil in a frying pan, add the garlic, onion and mustard seeds, and cook over medium heat for 5 minutes, or until the onion is golden. Add the asafoetida, cumin seeds, ground coriander and chilli, and cook for 2 minutes.

Add the onion mixture to the lentils and stir gently to combine. Add 125 ml (4 fl oz/½ cup) water, reduce the heat to low and cook for 5 minutes. Stir in the lemon juice and serve.

SERVES 4-6

Far left: Add the ginger slices and turmeric to the lentils and simmer.

Left: Stir the onion mixture gently through the lentil mixture.

Jungle Curry Prawns

Be warned: jungle curries are generally hot curries! Traditionally, there is no coconut to absorb the heat of the chillies. However, they usually also feature plenty of fresh spices and vegetables. The final flavour is aromatic, hot and salty, but not scorching.

JUNGLE CURRY PASTE
10–12 dried red chillies
1 teaspoon white pepper
4 red Asian shallots
4 garlic cloves
1 lemongrass stem, white part only, chopped
1 tablespoon finely chopped galangal
2 coriander (cilantro) roots
1 tablespoon finely chopped ginger
1 tablespoon dry-roasted shrimp paste

1 tablespoon peanut oil
1 garlic clove, crushed
1 tablespoon fish sauce
30 g (1 oz/¼ cup) ground candlenuts
300 ml (10½ fl oz) fish stock
1 tablespoon whisky
3 makrut (kaffir lime) leaves, torn
600 g (1 lb 5 oz) raw prawns (shrimp), peeled and deveined, tails intact
1 small carrot, quartered lengthways, sliced thinly on the diagonal
150 g (5½ oz) snake (yard-long) beans, cut into 2 cm (¾ in) lengths
50 g (1¾ oz/¼ cup) bamboo shoots
Thai basil, to serve

Soak the chillies in boiling water for 5 minutes, or until soft. Remove the stem and seeds, then chop. Put the chillies and the remaining curry paste ingredients in a food processor, or in a mortar with a pestle, and process or pound to a smooth paste. Add a little water if it is too thick.

Heat a wok over medium heat, add the oil and swirl to coat. Add the garlic and 3 tablespoons of the curry paste and cook, stirring, for 5 minutes. Add the fish sauce, ground candlenuts, fish stock, whisky, makrut leaves, prawns, carrot, beans and bamboo shoots. Bring to the boil, then reduce the heat and simmer for 5 minutes, or until the prawns and vegetables are cooked. Top with Thai basil and serve.

SERVES 6

Split the chillies then scrape away the seeds with a knife.

Sri Lankan Fried Pork Curry

This curry is interesting for the number of flavourings not often seen in western dishes. Fenugreek seeds are small, hard and ochre-coloured. They are powerfully scented and have a bitter taste, though this softens on cooking.

80 ml (2½ fl oz/⅓ cup) oil
1.25 kg (2 lb 12 oz) boned pork shoulder, cut into
   3 cm (1¼ in) cubes
1 large red onion, finely chopped
3–4 garlic cloves, crushed
1 tablespoon grated ginger
10 curry leaves

½ teaspoon fenugreek seeds
½ teaspoon chilli powder
6 cardamom pods, bruised
2½ tablespoons Sri Lankan curry powder
1 tablespoon white vinegar
3 tablespoons tamarind concentrate
270 ml (9½ fl oz) coconut cream

Heat half the oil in a large saucepan over high heat, add the meat and cook in batches for 6 minutes, or until well browned. Remove from the pan. Heat the remaining oil, add the onion and cook over medium heat for 5 minutes, or until lightly browned. Add the garlic and ginger, and cook for 2 minutes. Stir in the curry leaves, spices and curry powder, and cook for 2 minutes, or until fragrant. Stir in the vinegar and 1 teaspoon salt.

Return the meat to the pan, add the tamarind concentrate and 310 ml (10¾ fl oz/1¼ cups) water and simmer, covered, stirring occasionally, for 40–50 minutes, or until the meat is tender. Stir in the coconut cream and simmer, uncovered, for 15 minutes, or until the sauce has reduced and thickened a little. Serve immediately.

SERVES 6

Rogan Josh

This classic, superbly aromatic, slow-cooking curry originated in Persia, and travelled to Kashmir, in India's far north, under the Moghul empire. In Kashmir it was adapted and perfected, incorporating the local chillies: saffron and cardamom.

8 garlic cloves, crushed
3 teaspoons grated ginger
2 teaspoons ground cumin
1 teaspoon chilli powder
2 teaspoons paprika
2 teaspoons ground coriander
1 kg (2 lb 4 oz) boneless leg or shoulder of lamb, cut into 3 cm (1¼ in) cubes
3 tablespoons ghee or oil

1 onion, finely chopped
6 cardamom pods, bruised
4 cloves
2 Indian bay (cassia) leaves
1 cinnamon stick
185 g (6½ oz/¾ cup) Greek-style yoghurt
4 saffron threads, mixed with 2 tablespoons milk
¼ teaspoon garam masala

Mix the garlic, ginger, cumin, chilli powder, paprika and coriander in a large bowl. Add the meat and stir thoroughly to coat. Cover and marinate for at least 2 hours, or overnight, in the refrigerator.

Heat the ghee or oil in a flameproof casserole dish or karahi over low heat. Add the onion and cook for about 10 minutes, or until the onion is lightly browned. Remove from the dish.

Add the cardamom pods, cloves, bay leaves and cinnamon to the dish and fry for 1 minute. Turn the heat to high, add the meat and onion, then mix well and fry for 2 minutes. Stir well, then reduce the heat to low, cover and cook for 15 minutes.

Uncover and fry for another 3–5 minutes, or until the meat is quite dry. Add 100 ml (3½ fl oz) water, cover and cook for 5–7 minutes, until the water has evaporated and the oil separates and floats on the surface. Fry the meat for another 1–2 minutes, then add 250 ml (9 fl oz/1 cup) water. Cover and cook for 40–50 minutes, gently simmering until the meat is tender. The liquid will reduce quite a bit.

Stir in the yoghurt when the meat is almost tender, taking care not to allow the meat to catch on the base of the dish. Add the saffron and milk. Stir the mixture a few times to mix in the saffron. Season with salt to taste. Remove from the heat and sprinkle with the garam masala.

SERVES 6

Right: Coat the meat well in the mixed spices and leave to marinate.

Far right: Dry-fry the spices for 1 minute, or until they become aromatic.

Sri Lankan Eggplant Curry

There are many similarities between Indian and Sri Lankan cooking, but they are not interchangeable and their curry powders differ. Sri Lankan curry powder is made by roasting spices such as cumin, fennel and coriander and has a dark, intense flavour.

1 teaspoon ground turmeric
12 slender eggplants (aubergines), cut into
    4 cm (1½ in) rounds
oil for deep-frying, plus 2 tablespoons extra
2 onions, finely chopped
2 tablespoons Sri Lankan curry powder

2 garlic cloves, crushed
8 curry leaves, roughly chopped, plus extra whole leaves
    for garnish
½ teaspoon chilli powder
250 ml (9 fl oz/1 cup) coconut cream

Mix half the ground turmeric with 1 teaspoon salt and rub into the eggplant, ensuring the cut surfaces are well coated. Put in a colander and leave for 1 hour. Rinse well and put on crumpled paper towel to remove any excess moisture.

Fill a deep heavy-based saucepan one-third full of oil and heat to 180°C (350°F), or until a cube of bread dropped into the oil browns in 15 seconds. Cook the eggplant in batches for 1 minute, or until golden brown. Drain on crumpled paper towel.

Heat the extra oil in a large saucepan, add the onion and cook over medium heat for 5 minutes, or until browned. Add the curry powder, garlic, curry leaves, chilli powder, eggplant and remaining turmeric to the pan, and cook for 2 minutes. Stir in the coconut cream and 250 ml (9 fl oz/1 cup) water, and season with salt to taste. Reduce the heat and simmer over low heat for 3 minutes, or until the eggplant is fully cooked and the sauce has thickened slightly. Garnish with extra curry leaves.

SERVES 6

Far left: Rub the ground turmeric and salt into the eggplants' cut surfaces.

Left: Fry the eggplant in a deep saucepan until golden and tender.

CURRIED SQUID

This quick and simple curry packs quite a flavour punch. It features the round, earthy flavours of cumin and turmeric, alongside the fresh, sharper flavours of chilli, ginger and lime juice. Versions of this dish are eaten throughout Thailand and Singapore.

1 kg (2 lb 4 oz) squid
1 teaspoon cumin seeds
1 teaspoon coriander seeds
1 teaspoon chilli powder
1/2 teaspoon ground turmeric
2 tablespoons oil
1 onion, finely chopped

10 curry leaves, plus extra for garnish
1/2 teaspoon fenugreek seeds
4 garlic cloves, crushed
7 cm (2 3/4 in) piece ginger, grated
100 ml (3 1/2 fl oz) coconut cream
3 tablespoons lime juice

Pull the squid heads and tentacles out of their bodies, along with any innards, and discard. Peel off the skins. Rinse the bodies well, pulling out the clear quills, then cut the bodies into 2.5 cm (1 in) rings.

Dry-fry the cumin and coriander seeds in a frying pan over medium–high heat for 2–3 minutes, or until fragrant. Allow to cool. Using a mortar with a pestle, or a spice grinder, crush or grind to a powder. Mix the ground cumin and coriander with

the chilli powder and ground turmeric. Add the squid and mix well.

In a heavy-based frying pan, heat the oil and fry the onion until lightly browned. Add the curry leaves, fenugreek, garlic, ginger and coconut cream. Bring slowly to the boil. Add the squid, then stir well. Simmer for 2–3 minutes, or until cooked and tender. Stir in the lime juice, season and serve garnished with curry leaves.

SERVES 4

Finely grind the peppercorns in a mortar or use a spice grinder.

Chapter 3

HOT AND SOUR

The combination of hot and sour is a particularly happy one, with the sour elements adding an extra layer of flavour and fragrance to a hot dish. Sour ingredients also add textural interest and further complexity can be added with the use of rich, creamy coconut milk. As with all curries, balance is the key.

Pork Vindaloo

The Portuguese first introduced this stew to Goa. The locals adopted it but, finding it lacking slightly in flavour, proceeded to adapt it, adding spices, extra garlic and a hefty quantity of chillies. The result is vindaloo, famed for its heat and spiciness.

1 kg (2 lb 4 oz) pork fillet
3 tablespoons oil
2 onions, finely chopped
4 garlic cloves, crushed

1 tablespoon finely chopped ginger
1 tablespoon garam masala
2 teaspoons brown mustard seeds
4 tablespoons ready-made vindaloo paste

Trim the pork fillet of any excess fat and sinew and cut into bite-sized pieces.

Heat the oil in a saucepan, add the meat in small batches and cook over medium heat for 5–7 minutes, or until browned. Remove from the pan.

Add the onion, garlic, ginger, garam masala and mustard seeds to the pan, and cook, stirring, for 5 minutes, or until the onion is soft.

Return all the meat to the pan, add the vindaloo paste and cook, stirring, for 2 minutes. Add 625 ml (21½ fl oz/2½ cups) water and bring to the boil. Reduce the heat and simmer, covered, for 1½ hours, or until the meat is tender.

SERVES 4

Balinese Seafood Curry

The chilli arrived in Bali fairly recently — with the Portuguese in the sixteenth century — but it has found its way into most dishes. Balinese cuisine is renowned for its spicy and complex flavours, its love of fish and careful preparation of the spice blend.

CURRY PASTE
1 tablespoon coriander seeds
1 teaspoon shrimp paste
2 tomatoes
5 red chillies
5 garlic cloves, crushed
2 lemongrass stems, white part only, chopped
1 tablespoon ground almonds
1/4 teaspoon ground nutmeg
1 teaspoon ground turmeric
60 g (2 1/4 oz/ 1/4 cup) tamarind purée

3 tablespoons lime juice
250 g (9 oz) skinless, firm white fish fillets, cut into
  3 cm (1 1/4 in) cubes
3 tablespoons oil
2 red onions, chopped
2 red chillies, seeded, sliced
400 g (14 oz), raw prawns (shrimp) peeled and deveined,
  tails intact
250 g (9 oz) squid tubes, cut into 1 cm (1/2 in) rings
125 ml (4 fl oz/ 1/2 cup) fish stock
shredded Thai basil, to serve

Dry-fry the coriander seeds and the shrimp paste wrapped in some foil in a frying pan over medium–high heat for 2–3 minutes, or until fragrant. Allow to cool. Using a mortar with a pestle, or a spice grinder, crush or grind the coriander seeds to a powder.

Score a cross in the base of the tomatoes, place in a heatproof bowl and cover with boiling water. Leave to stand for 30 seconds, then transfer to cold water and peel the skin away from the cross. Cut the tomatoes in half and scoop out the seeds. Discard the seeds and roughly chop the tomato flesh.

Put the crushed coriander seeds, the shrimp paste and tomato with the remaining curry paste ingredients in a food processor, or in a mortar with a pestle, and process or pound to a smooth paste.

Put the lime juice in a bowl and season with salt and freshly ground black pepper. Add the fish, toss to coat well and leave to marinate for 20 minutes.

Heat the oil in a saucepan or wok, add the onion, sliced red chilli and curry paste, and cook, stirring occasionally, over low heat for 10 minutes, or until fragrant. Add the fish and prawns, and stir to coat in the curry paste mixture. Cook for 3 minutes, or until the prawns just turn pink, then add the squid and cook for 1 minute.

Add the stock and bring to the boil, then reduce the heat and simmer for 2 minutes, or until the seafood is cooked and tender. Season to taste with salt and freshly ground black pepper. Top with the shredded basil leaves.

SERVES 6

Malaysian Nonya Chicken Curry

In the fifteenth century, the Strait of Malacca was the favoured route of Chinese traders to Arabia and India. Many settled in the area and married the local women. A unique cuisine developed, which blended Chinese techniques and Malaysian spices.

CURRY PASTE
1/2 teaspoon shrimp paste
2 red onions, chopped
4 red chillies, seeded
4 garlic cloves, crushed
2 lemongrass stems, white part only, sliced
3 cm (1 1/4 in) cube galangal, sliced
8 makrut (kaffir lime) leaves, roughly chopped
1 teaspoon ground turmeric

2 tablespoons oil
750 g (1 lb 10 oz) chicken thigh fillets, cut into
    bite-sized pieces
400 ml (14 fl oz) coconut milk
3 1/2 tablespoons tamarind purée
1 tablespoon fish sauce
3 makrut (kaffir lime) leaves, shredded

Dry-fry the shrimp paste wrapped in some foil in a frying pan over medium–high heat for 2–3 minutes, or until fragrant. Allow to cool.

Put the shrimp paste with the remaining curry paste ingredients in a food processor, or in a mortar with a pestle, and process or pound to a smooth paste.

Heat a wok or large saucepan over high heat, add the oil and swirl to coat the side. Add the curry

paste and cook, stirring occasionally, over low heat for 8–10 minutes, or until fragrant. Add the chicken and stir-fry with the paste for 2–3 minutes.

Add the coconut milk, tamarind purée and fish sauce to the wok, and simmer, stirring occasionally, for 15–20 minutes, or until the chicken is tender. Garnish with the shredded makrut leaves and serve.

SERVES 4

Far left: Put the paste ingredients in a food processor or mortar.

Left: Process or pound the mixture until a smooth paste is formed.

Goan Fish Curry

Goa is situated on India's southwest coast where seafood is a staple ingredient. The other favourite ingredient is coconut, and few dishes are without it. Dishes, including this one, are simple and pleasantly spicy with chillies, ginger, turmeric and tamarind.

3 tablespoons oil
1 large onion, finely chopped
4–5 garlic cloves, crushed
2 teaspoons grated ginger
4–6 dried red chillies
1 tablespoon coriander seeds
2 teaspoons cumin seeds
1 teaspoon ground turmeric
1/4 teaspoon chilli powder
30 g (1 oz/1/3 cup) desiccated coconut

270 ml (9 1/2 fl oz) coconut milk
2 tomatoes, peeled and chopped
2 tablespoons tamarind purée
1 tablespoon white vinegar
6 curry leaves
1 kg (2 lb 4 oz) firm white fish fillets, skinless, cut into
    8 cm (3 1/4 in) pieces

Heat the oil in a large saucepan. Add the onion and cook, stirring, over low heat for 10 minutes, or until softened and lightly golden. Add the garlic and ginger, and cook for a further 2 minutes.

Dry-fry the dried chillies, coriander seeds, cumin seeds, ground turmeric, chilli powder and desiccated coconut in a frying pan over medium–high heat for 2–3 minutes, or until fragrant. Allow to cool. Using a mortar with a pestle, or a spice grinder, crush or grind to a powder.

Add the spice mixture, coconut milk, tomato, tamarind, vinegar and curry leaves to the onion mixture. Stir to mix thoroughly, add 250 ml (9 fl oz/1 cup) water and simmer, stirring frequently, for 10 minutes, or until the tomato has softened and the mixture has thickened slightly.

Add the fish and cook, covered, over low heat for 10 minutes, or until cooked through. Stir gently once or twice during cooking and add a little water if the mixture is too thick.

SERVES 6

Far left: Dry-fry the spices and desiccated coconut until aromatic.

Left: Use a mortar with a pestle or spice grinder to grind the spices.

BEEF BALLS WITH PICKLED GARLIC

This dish involves little preparation, making it a welcome choice when you feel like a curry but can't be bothered with the grinding and roasting. Pickled garlic has a sweet–sour flavour and is used in curries as a means of balancing other flavours.

MEATBALLS
450 g (1 lb) minced (ground) beef
3 garlic cloves, crushed
1 teaspoon white pepper
1 small handful coriander (cilantro) leaves, chopped
1 small handful Thai basil, chopped
1 spring onion (scallion), finely chopped
3 teaspoons fish sauce
1 egg

3 tablespoons oil
3 tablespoons ready-made green curry paste or see
　recipe on page 120
3 tablespoons finely chopped ginger
1 ½ teaspoons ground turmeric
3 tablespoons fish sauce
3 makrut (kaffir lime) leaves
2 ½ tablespoons tamarind purée
3 tablespoons chopped pickled garlic
1 ½ tablespoons shaved palm sugar (jaggery)

To make the meatballs, combine all the ingredients together well. Then, taking a tablespoon at a time, roll the mixture into small balls. You should have about 24 balls.

Heat the oil in a heavy-based saucepan over medium heat and add the curry paste, ginger and turmeric and cook, stirring frequently for about 5 minutes, or until fragrant.

Add the fish sauce, makrut leaves and tamarind. Bring to the boil then cover, reduce to a simmer and cook for 5 minutes. Add the meatballs, pickled garlic and palm sugar and simmer for 15 minutes, or until meatballs are cooked through.

SERVES 4

Far left: Roll tablespoons of the mince mixture into 24 balls.

Left: Add the meatballs to the sauce and simmer until cooked through.

Malaysian Hot and Sour Pineapple Curry

Pineapple adds a touch of tart sweetness to curries and is popular in vegetarian meals.
Here, it is mixed with hot chillies, creamy coconut and the mellow warmth of cloves
and cinnamon to produce a refreshing dish that is a little bit sweet and a little bit spicy.

1 semi-ripe pineapple, cored, cut into chunks
½ teaspoon ground turmeric
1 star anise
1 cinnamon stick, broken into small pieces
7 cloves
7 cardamom pods, bruised
1 tablespoon oil

1 onion, finely chopped
1 teaspoon grated ginger
1 garlic clove, crushed
5 red chillies, chopped
1 tablespoon sugar
3 tablespoons coconut cream

Put the pineapple in a saucepan, cover with water
and add the turmeric. Put the star anise,
cinnamon, cloves and cardamom pods on a square
of muslin, and tie securely with string. Add to the
pan and cook over medium heat for 10 minutes.
Squeeze the bag to extract any flavour, then
discard. Reserve the cooking liquid.

Heat the oil in a frying pan, add the onion,
ginger, garlic and chilli, and cook, stirring, for
1–2 minutes, or until fragrant. Add the pineapple
and the cooking liquid, sugar and salt to taste.
Cook for 2 minutes, then stir in the coconut
cream. Cook, stirring, over low heat for
3–5 minutes, or until the sauce thickens. Serve
this curry hot or cold.

SERVES 6

Tamarind Fish Curry

Tamarind is widely used for its sweet–sour flavour and souring properties. Here, the tamarind is balanced by full-bodied peppercorns, cumin and coriander; made aromatic with pungent saffron and sweet cardamom; and creamy with thick yoghurt.

600 g (1 lb 5 oz) skinless, firm white fish fillets
1 teaspoon turmeric
pinch powdered saffron
3 garlic cloves, crushed
2 teaspoons lemon juice
1 teaspoon cumin seeds
2 tablespoons coriander seeds
1 teaspoon white peppercorns
4 cardamom pods, bruised
2½ tablespoons finely chopped ginger

2 red chillies, finely sliced
2 tablespoons oil
1 onion, chopped
1 red capsicum (pepper), cut into 2 cm (³/4 in) squares
1 green capsicum (pepper), cut into 2 cm (³/4 in) squares
4 Roma (plum) tomatoes, diced
2 tablespoons tamarind purée
185 g (6½ oz/³/4 cup) plain yoghurt
2 tablespoons chopped coriander (cilantro) leaves

Rinse the fish fillets and pat dry. Prick the fillets with a fork. Combine the turmeric, saffron, garlic, lemon juice and 1 teaspoon of salt then rub over the fish fillets. Refrigerate for 2–3 hours.

Dry-fry the cumin seeds, coriander seeds, peppercorns and cardamom in a frying pan over medium–high heat for 2–3 minutes, or until fragrant. Allow to cool. Using a mortar with a pestle, or a spice grinder, crush or grind to a powder and combine with the ginger and chillies.

Heat the oil in a heavy-based saucepan over medium heat and add the chopped onion, red and green capsicum, and ground spice mix. Cook gently for 10 minutes, or until aromatic and the onion is transparent. Increase heat to high, add the diced tomatoes, 250 ml (9 fl oz/1 cup) of water and the tamarind purée. Bring to the boil then reduce to a simmer and cook for 20 minutes.

Rinse the paste off the fish and chop into 3 cm (1¼ in) pieces. Add to the pan and continue to simmer for 10 minutes. Stir in the yoghurt and chopped coriander and serve.

SERVES 4

Right; Rub the saffron mixture into the fish fillets and leave for 2–3 hours.

Far right: Add the onion, capsicum and spice mix to the saucepan.

PORK AND BITTER MELON CURRY

This is an impressive looking curry, with its stuffed bitter melon commanding attention. In this dish, this distinctive vegetable is balanced by other strong flavours, including pork, garlic and chillies. Despite its name, bitter melon is actually quite delicious.

6 bitter melon, about 700 g (1 lb 9 oz) total
2 tablespoons sugar

PORK FILLING
250 g (9 oz) minced (ground) pork
1 teaspoon chopped ginger
½ teaspoon white peppercorns, crushed
1 garlic clove, crushed
1 spring onion (scallion), finely chopped
1 teaspoon paprika
2 tablespoons finely chopped water chestnuts
2 makrut (kaffir lime) leaves, thinly sliced

1 ½ tablespoons crushed peanuts
1 small handful coriander (cilantro) leaves, chopped
1 tablespoon shaved palm sugar (jaggery)
1 tablespoon fish sauce

3 tablespoons oil
2 tablespoons ready-made red curry paste or see recipe
    on page 20
1 tablespoon shaved palm sugar (jaggery)
2 tablespoons fish sauce
250 ml (9 fl oz/1 cup) coconut cream
4 makrut (kaffir lime) leaves

Discard the ends of the bitter melon then cut into 2.5 cm (1 in) slices. Hollow out the fibrous centre membrane and seeds with a small knife, leaving the outside rings intact. Bring 750 ml (26 fl oz/3 cups) water to the boil with the sugar and 3 teaspoons salt. Blanch the melon for 2 minutes and drain.

Combine all ingredients for the pork filling. Pack this into the melon pieces. Heat 2 tablespoons of the oil in a heavy-based saucepan over low heat and add the melon, cooking for 3 minutes on each side, or until pork is golden and sealed. Set aside.

Add the remaining oil to the pan with the red curry paste. Stir for 3 minutes, or until aromatic. Add the palm sugar and fish sauce and stir until dissolved. Add the coconut cream, 250 ml (9 fl oz/1 cup) water and makrut leaves. Simmer for 5 minutes, then carefully add the bitter melon. Continue simmering, turning pork halfway through, for 20 minutes, or until pork is cooked and the melon is tender.

Note: Telegraph (long) cucumbers can be used instead of bitter melon.

SERVES 4

Far left: Cut the bitter melon into slices and hollow out the centre.

Left: Pack the pork filling into the bitter melon slices.

HOT AND SOUR EGGPLANT CURRY

Eggplant (aubergine) goes particularly well with coriander, cumin and coconut — rich, warm flavours — but is surprisingly amenable to a wide range of ingredients, such as the curry-scented fenugreek and anise-flavoured fennel used in this dish.

1 large (about 500 g/1 lb 2 oz) eggplant (aubergine)
2 small tomatoes
2 tablespoons oil
3 teaspoons fenugreek seeds
3 teaspoons fennel seeds
4 garlic cloves, crushed
1 large onion, finely diced
4 curry leaves

1 ½ tablespoons ground coriander
2 teaspoons turmeric
125 ml (4 fl oz/½ cup) tomato juice
2 tablespoons tamarind purée
2 red chillies, finely sliced
125 ml (4 fl oz/½ cup) coconut cream
1 handful coriander (cilantro) leaves, chopped

Cut the eggplant into 2 cm (¾ in) cubes. Sprinkle with ½ teaspoon salt and set aside for 1 hour. Drain and rinse.

Chop the tomatoes into rough dice. Heat the oil in a heavy-based saucepan over medium heat. Add the fenugreek and fennel seeds. When they start to crackle, add the garlic, onion and curry leaves and cook for 3–5 minutes or until onion is transparent.

Add the eggplant and stir for 6 minutes, or until it begins to soften. Add the ground spices, tomatoes, tomato juice, tamarind and sliced fresh chillies.

Bring to the boil, then reduce to a simmer, cover and continue to cook for about 35 minutes, or until eggplant is very soft. Stir in the coconut cream and coriander and season to taste.

SERVES 4

Far left: Chop the tomatoes into a rough dice, keeping the skin and seeds.

Left: When the eggplant is very soft, stir in the coconut cream.

Balti-Style Lamb

Baltistan may lie high in the mountains of north Pakistan, but Birmingham, England, has become the international launch pad of balti cuisine. Distinctive for its use of the two-handled karahi pot, it also features its own fragrant masala paste.

1 kg (2 lb 4 oz) lamb leg steaks, cut into 3 cm (1 ¼ in) cubes
5 tablespoons ready-made balti masala paste
2 tablespoons ghee or oil
3 garlic cloves, crushed

1 tablespoon garam masala
1 large onion, finely chopped
2 tablespoons chopped coriander (cilantro) leaves, plus extra for garnish

Preheat the oven to 190°C (375°F/Gas 5). Put the meat, 1 tablespoon of the balti masala paste and 375 ml (13 fl oz/1½ cups) boiling water in a large casserole dish or karahi, and combine. Cook, covered, in the oven for 30–40 minutes, or until almost cooked through. Drain, reserving the stock.

Heat the ghee or oil in a wok, add the garlic and garam masala, and stir-fry over medium heat for 1 minute. Add the onion and cook for 5–7 minutes, or until the onion is soft and golden brown. Increase the heat, add the remaining balti

masala paste and the lamb. Cook for 5 minutes to brown the meat. Slowly add the reserved stock and simmer over low heat, stirring occasionally, for 15 minutes.

Add the chopped coriander leaves and 185 ml (6 fl oz/¾ cup) water and simmer for 15 minutes, or until the meat is tender and the sauce has thickened slightly. Season with salt and freshly ground black pepper and garnish with extra coriander leaves.

SERVES 4

Duck and Coconut Curry

The use of sour vinegar in a curry may seem an unusual addition, but it can provide an excellent foil for rich coconut milk and fatty meat such as duck. In India, it is often found in regional cooking that has been influenced by other cultures.

CURRY PASTE
1½ teaspoons coriander seeds
1 teaspoon cardamom seeds
1 teaspoon fenugreek seeds
1 teaspoon brown mustard seeds
10 black peppercorns
1 red onion, chopped
2 garlic cloves, crushed
4 red chillies, seeded, chopped
2 coriander (cilantro) roots, chopped

2 teaspoons grated ginger
2 teaspoons garam masala
¼ teaspoon ground turmeric
2 teaspoons tamarind purée

6 duck breast fillets
1 red onion, sliced
125 ml (4 fl oz/½ cup) white vinegar
500 ml (17 fl oz/2 cups) coconut milk
1 small handful coriander (cilantro) leaves

Dry-fry the coriander, cardamom, fenugreek and mustard seeds in a frying pan over medium–high heat for 2–3 minutes, or until fragrant. Allow to cool. Using a mortar with a pestle, or a spice grinder, crush or grind the spices with the black peppercorns to a powder.

Put the ground spices with the remaining curry paste ingredients in a food processor, or in a mortar with a pestle, and make a smooth paste.

Trim any excess fat from the duck fillets, then place, skin side down, in a large saucepan and cook over medium heat for 10 minutes, or until the skin is brown and any remaining fat has melted. Turn the fillets over and cook for 5 minutes, or until tender. Remove and drain on paper towel.

Reserve 1 tablespoon duck fat, discard the remaining fat. Add the onion and cook for 5 minutes, then add the curry paste and stir over low heat for 10 minutes, or until fragrant.

Return the duck to the pan and stir to coat with the paste. Stir in the vinegar, coconut milk, 1 teaspoon salt and 125 ml (4 fl oz/½ cup) water. Simmer, covered, for 45 minutes, or until the fillets are tender. Stir in the coriander leaves just before serving.

SERVES 6

Right: Process the onion, garlic, spices and tamarind until smooth.

Far right: Trim the excess fat from the duck fillets before adding to the pan.

Sour Lamb and Bamboo Curry

Bamboo shoots are used mainly in Southeast Asian cooking. When fresh, they have a lovely crisp, nutty bitterness to them. They are available in Asian food stores, but the tinned variety makes an acceptable substitute.

CURRY PASTE
1 teaspoon white peppercorns
1 teaspoon shrimp paste
30 g (1 oz) dried shrimp
6 spring onions (scallions), sliced
60 g (2¼ oz) sliced jalapeño chillies (in brine)
2 lemongrass stems, white part only, thinly sliced
6 garlic cloves, crushed
4 coriander (cilantro) roots, chopped
2 teaspoons ground galangal
1 teaspoon chilli powder
80 ml (2½ fl oz/⅓ cup) fish sauce
80 ml (2½ fl oz/⅓ cup) lime juice
1 teaspoon ground turmeric

500 g (1 lb 2 oz) boneless lamb leg, trimmed
    of excess fat
1 tablespoon oil
1 tablespoon shaved palm sugar (jaggery)
250 ml (9 fl oz/1 cup) coconut cream
60 g (2¼ oz/¼ cup) tamarind purée
1½ tablespoons fish sauce
400 g (14 oz) tinned bamboo shoot pieces, cut into
    thick wedges
200 g (7 oz) green beans, cut into 4 cm (1½ in) lengths

Dry-fry the peppercorns and the shrimp paste wrapped in some foil in a frying pan over medium–high heat for 2–3 minutes, or until fragrant. Allow to cool. Using a mortar with a pestle, or a spice grinder, crush or grind to a powder. Process the dried shrimp in a food processor until it becomes very finely shredded — forming a 'floss'.

Put the crushed peppercorns, shrimp paste and dried shrimp with the remaining curry paste ingredients in a food processor, or in a mortar with a pestle, and process or pound to a smooth paste.

Slice the lamb into strips 5 cm x 2 cm (2 in x ¾ in) and 3 mm (⅛ in) thick. Heat the oil in a heavy-based casserole dish over medium heat and add 2–3 tablespoons of paste. Stir constantly, adding the palm sugar. When the palm sugar has dissolved add the lamb, stirring for about 7 minutes, or until lightly golden.

Add the coconut cream, 250 ml (9 fl oz/1 cup) water, tamarind, fish sauce and bamboo. Bring to the boil then reduce heat and simmer for about 20 minutes, or until tender. Add the beans and simmer for a further 3 minutes. Season to taste and serve.

SERVES 4

Thai Hot and Sour Prawn and Pumpkin Curry

Flavoured with red curry paste, perfumed by makrut (kaffir lime) leaves, and seasoned with tamarind, fish sauce, lime juice and chillies, this delicious curry is a real meal-in-a-bowl. The flavours are well-balanced, with a bit of bite and a lovely tangy taste.

250 g (9 oz) jap pumpkin (kent squash)
1 Lebanese (short) cucumber
400 ml (14 fl oz/1²/₃ cups) coconut cream (do not shake the tin)
1½ tablespoons ready-made red curry paste or see recipe on page 20
3 tablespoons fish sauce
2 tablespoons shaved palm sugar (jaggery)
400 g (14 oz) tinned straw mushrooms, drained

500 g (1 lb 2 oz) raw prawns (shrimp), peeled, deveined, tails intact
2 tablespoons tamarind purée
2 red chillies, chopped
1 tablespoon lime juice
4 makrut (kaffir lime) leaves
4 coriander (cilantro) roots, chopped
1 small handful bean sprouts, to serve
1 small handful coriander (cilantro) leaves, to serve

Peel the pumpkin and chop into 2 cm (¾ in) cubes. Peel and cut the cucumber in half lengthways, then scrape out the seeds with a teaspoon and thinly slice.

Put the thick coconut cream from the top of the tin in a saucepan, bring to a rapid simmer over medium heat, stirring occasionally, and cook for 5–10 minutes, or until the mixture 'splits' (the oil starts to separate). Add the paste and stir for 2–3 minutes, or until fragrant. Add the fish sauce and palm sugar and stir until dissolved.

Add the remaining coconut cream, pumpkin, and 3 tablespoons of water, cover and bring to boil. Reduce to a simmer and cook for 10 minutes, or until pumpkin is just starting to become tender. Add the straw mushrooms, prawns, cucumber, tamarind, chilli, lime juice, makrut leaves and coriander roots. Cover, increase the heat and bring to the boil again before reducing to a simmer and cooking for 3–5 minutes, or until the prawns are just cooked through. Garnish with bean sprouts and coriander leaves.

SERVES 4

Chapter 4

AROMATIC

Pepper, chillies and turmeric are all aromatic, but that is not what first comes to mind when thinking about the impact they have on a curry. On the other hand, fresh Thai basil and coriander (cilantro) leaves, cloves and nutmeg all suggest dishes whose aroma — be it sweet, clean, sharp or pungent — immediately invites and seduces.

SPICED CHICKEN WITH ALMONDS

This is a simple and aromatic dish, with little of the sharpness found in many curries. Almonds were introduced to India by the Moghul emperors and remain associated with sumptuous dining. Here they are used both in the sauce and garnish.

3 tablespoons oil
30 g (1 oz/¼ cup) slivered almonds
2 red onions, finely chopped
4–6 garlic cloves, crushed
1 tablespoon grated ginger
4 cardamom pods, bruised
4 cloves
1 teaspoon ground cumin

1 teaspoon ground coriander
1 teaspoon ground turmeric
½ teaspoon chilli powder
1 kg (2 lb 4 oz) chicken thigh fillets, trimmed
2 large, peeled, chopped tomatoes
1 cinnamon stick
100 g (3½ oz/1 cup) ground almonds

Heat 1 tablespoon oil in a large saucepan. Add the almonds and cook over low heat for 15 seconds, or until lightly golden brown. Remove and drain on crumpled paper towel.

Heat the remaining oil, add the onion, and cook, stirring, for 8 minutes, or until golden brown. Add the garlic and ginger and cook, stirring, for 2 minutes, then stir in the spices. Reduce the heat to low and cook for 2 minutes, or until aromatic.

Add the chicken and cook, stirring constantly, for 5 minutes, or until well coated with the spices and starting to colour.

Stir in the tomato, cinnamon stick, ground almonds and 250 ml (9 fl oz/1 cup) hot water. Simmer, covered, over low heat for 1 hour, or until the chicken is cooked through and tender. Stir often and add a little more water, if needed.

Leave the pan to stand, covered, for 30 minutes for the flavours to develop, then remove the cinnamon stick. Scatter the slivered almonds over the top and serve.

SERVES 6

Far left: Toss the chicken pieces in the spices, coating well.

Left: Add the tomato, cinnamon and ground almonds and simmer.

CREAMY PRAWN CURRY

Creamy, yes, but also fragrant with cloves, cardamom, cinnamon and Indian bay leaves. Make sure you use Indian bay leaves and not the European variety. More accurately called cassia leaves, they are spicy and refreshing, with a sweet, woody aroma.

500 g (1 lb 2 oz) tiger prawns (shrimp), peeled, deveined, with tails intact
1½ tablespoons lemon juice
3 tablespoons oil
½ onion, finely chopped
½ teaspoon ground turmeric
1 cinnamon stick

4 cloves
7 cardamom pods, bruised
5 Indian bay (cassia) leaves
2 cm (¾ in) piece ginger, grated
3 garlic cloves, crushed
1 teaspoon chilli powder
170 ml (5½ fl oz/⅔ cup) coconut milk

Put the prawns in a bowl, add the lemon juice, then toss together and leave them for 5 minutes. Rinse the prawns under running cold water and pat dry with paper towel.

Heat the oil in a heavy-based frying pan and fry the onion until lightly browned. Add the turmeric, cinnamon, cloves, cardamom, bay leaves, ginger and garlic, and fry for 1 minute. Add the chilli powder, coconut milk, and salt to taste, and slowly bring to the boil. Reduce the heat and simmer for 2 minutes.

Add the prawns, return to the boil, then reduce the heat and simmer for 5 minutes, or until the prawns are cooked through and the sauce is thick.

SERVES 4

Right: Add the spices to the browned onion and cook until fragrant.

Far right: Simmer the prawns gently until just curled and cooked through.

PORK AND CARDAMOM CURRY

Tender, sweet pork fillet is perfect for this dish: it is fat-free, so needs an initial brief cooking to seal in the juices, but then will cook fairly quickly in the curry. The spices combine to give this dish a lovely warm, exotic flavour.

CURRY PASTE

10 cardamom pods
6 cm (2½ in) piece ginger, chopped
3 garlic cloves, crushed
2 teaspoons black peppercorns
1 cinnamon stick
1 onion, finely sliced
1 teaspoon ground cumin
1 teaspoon ground coriander
1 teaspoon garam masala

3 tablespoons oil
1 kg (2 lb 4 oz) pork fillet, thinly sliced
2 tomatoes, finely diced
125 ml (4 fl oz/½ cup) chicken stock
125 ml (4 fl oz/½ cup) coconut milk

Lightly crush the cardamom pods with the flat side of a heavy knife. Remove the seeds, discarding the pods. Put the seeds and the remaining curry paste ingredients in a food processor, or in a mortar with a pestle, and process or pound to a smooth paste.

Put 2½ tablespoons of oil in a large heavy-based frying pan, and fry the pork in batches until browned, then set aside. Add the remaining oil to the pan, then add the curry paste and cook over medium–high heat for 3–4 minutes, or until aromatic. Add the tomato, chicken stock and coconut milk, and simmer covered over low–medium heat for 15 minutes. While cooking, skim any oil that comes to the surface and discard.

Add the pork to the sauce, and simmer uncovered for 5 minutes, or until cooked. Season well to taste and serve.

SERVES 4

Dum Aloo

In India, 'dum' — 'to breathe in' — means to cook by steaming. The traditional method was to fill a pot with ingredients, seal the lid with dough and set the pot over coals. The food would slowly and delicately cook in its own steam and juices.

CURRY PASTE

4 cardamom pods
1 teaspoon grated ginger
2 garlic cloves, crushed
3 red chillies
1 teaspoon cumin seeds
40 g (1 ½ oz/ ¼ cup) cashew nuts
1 tablespoon white poppy seeds
1 cinnamon stick
6 cloves

1 kg (2 lb 4 oz) all-purpose potatoes, cubed
2 onions, roughly chopped
2 tablespoons oil
½ teaspoon ground turmeric
1 teaspoon besan (chickpea flour)
250 g (9 oz/1 cup) plain yoghurt
coriander (cilantro) leaves, to garnish

Lightly crush the cardamom pods with the flat side of a heavy knife. Remove the seeds, discarding the pods. Put the seeds and the remaining curry paste ingredients in a food processor, or in a mortar with a pestle, and process or pound to a smooth paste.

Bring a large saucepan of lightly salted water to the boil. Add the potato and cook for 5–6 minutes, or until just tender, then drain.

Put the onions in a food processor and process in short bursts until it is finely chopped but not puréed. Heat the oil in a large saucepan, add the onion and cook over low heat for 5 minutes. Add the curry paste and cook, stirring, for a further 5 minutes, or until fragrant. Stir in the potato, turmeric, salt to taste and 250 ml (9 fl oz/1 cup) cold water.

Reduce the heat and simmer, tightly covered, for 10 minutes, or until the potato is cooked but not breaking up and the sauce has thickened slightly.

Combine the besan with the yoghurt, add to the potato mixture and cook, stirring, over low heat for 5 minutes, or until thickened again. Garnish with the coriander leaves and serve.

SERVES 6

Right: Lightly crush the cardamom pods to release the seeds.

Far right: Stir in the yoghurt mixture and cook until thickened.

Indonesian Chicken in Coconut Milk

This heady dish perfectly conjures up Indonesia's tropical climate and produce. Curries are typically rich, relying on ingredients such as pepper, galangal, coriander and shrimp paste for hot, tangy and salty elements.

CURRY PASTE
2 teaspoons coriander seeds
1/2 teaspoon cumin seeds
2 teaspoons white peppercorns
1/2 teaspoon shrimp paste
30 g (1 oz) dried shrimp
2 lemongrass stems, white part only, sliced
2 red onions, chopped
3 garlic cloves, crushed
1 tablespoon grated ginger

2 1/2 tablespoons grated galangal
1/4 teaspoon ground nutmeg
1/4 teaspoon ground cloves

560 ml (19 1/4 fl oz/2 1/4 cups) coconut cream
1.5 kg (3 lb 5 oz) chicken, cut into 8–10 pieces
800 ml (28 fl oz/3 1/4 cups) coconut milk
2 tablespoons tamarind purée
1 tablespoon white vinegar
1 cinnamon stick

Dry-fry the coriander seeds, cumin seeds, white peppercorns and the shrimp paste wrapped in some foil in a frying pan over medium–high heat for 2–3 minutes, or until fragrant. Allow to cool. Using a mortar with a pestle, or a spice grinder, crush or grind the coriander, cumin and peppercorns to a powder. Process the shrimp in a food processor until it becomes very finely shredded — forming a 'floss'.

Put the crushed spices and the shrimp with the remaining curry paste ingredients in a food processor, or in a mortar with a pestle, and process or pound to a smooth paste.

Heat a large saucepan or wok over medium heat, add the coconut cream and curry paste, and cook, stirring, for 20 minutes, or until thick and oily.

Add the chicken and the remaining ingredients and simmer gently for 50 minutes, or until the chicken is tender. Season to taste and serve immediately.

SERVES 6

THAI GREEN CHICKEN CURRY

This dish is a classic of Thai cooking. It is hot and fragrant from the curry paste and perfumed with makrut (kaffir lime) leaves and Thai basil. Green pastes can vary, but they should be pungent rather than piercingly hot.

GREEN CURRY PASTE
1 teaspoon white peppercorns
2 tablespoons coriander seeds
1 teaspoon cumin seeds
2 teaspoons shrimp paste
1 teaspoon sea salt
4 lemongrass stems, white part only, finely sliced
2 teaspoons chopped galangal
1 makrut (kaffir lime) leaf, finely shredded
1 tablespoon chopped coriander (cilantro) root
5 red Asian shallots, chopped
10 garlic cloves, crushed
16 long green chillies, seeded, chopped

500 ml (17 fl oz/2 cups) coconut cream (do not shake the tins)
2 tablespoons shaved palm sugar (jaggery)
2 tablespoons fish sauce
4 makrut (kaffir lime) leaves, finely shredded
1 kg (2 lb 4 oz) chicken thigh or breast fillets, cut into thick strips
200 g (7 oz) bamboo shoots, cut into thick strips
100 g (3½ oz) snake (yard-long) beans, cut into 5 cm (2 in) lengths
1 handful Thai basil

Dry-fry the peppercorns, coriander seeds, cumin seeds and shrimp paste wrapped in foil in a frying pan over medium–high heat for 2–3 minutes, or until fragrant. Allow to cool. Using a mortar with a pestle, or a spice grinder, crush or grind the peppercorns, coriander and cumin to a powder.

Put the shrimp paste and ground spices with the remaining curry paste ingredients in a food processor, or in a mortar with a pestle, and process or pound to a smooth paste.

Put the thick coconut cream from the top of the tins in a saucepan, bring to a rapid simmer over medium heat, stirring occasionally, and cook for 5–10 minutes, or until the mixture 'splits' (the oil starts to separate).

Add 4 tablespoons of the green curry paste, then simmer for 15 minutes, or until fragrant. Add the palm sugar, fish sauce and makrut leaves to the pan.

Stir in the remaining coconut cream and the chicken, bamboo shoots and beans, and simmer for 15 minutes, or until the chicken is tender. Stir in the Thai basil and serve.

SERVES 4–6

Fish Koftas in Tomato Curry Sauce

Koftas were originally invented by the Arabs and have proved to be immensely versatile. In this dish, both the kofta and the sauce are quite aromatic; the sauce is slightly sweet and earthy, while the kofta are rich and spicy.

KOFTAS

750 g (1 lb 10 oz) firm white fish fillets, roughly skinless,
1 onion, chopped
2–3 garlic cloves, crushed
1 tablespoon grated ginger
4 tablespoons chopped coriander (cilantro) leaves
1 teaspoon garam masala
1/4 teaspoon chilli powder
1 egg, lightly beaten
oil, for shallow-frying

TOMATO CURRY SAUCE

2 tablespoons oil
1 large onion, finely chopped
3–4 garlic cloves, crushed
1 tablespoon grated ginger
1 teaspoon ground turmeric
1 teaspoon ground cumin
1 teaspoon ground coriander
1 teaspoon garam masala
1/4 teaspoon chilli powder
800 g (1 lb 12 oz) tinned crushed tomatoes
3 tablespoons chopped coriander (cilantro) leaves, plus extra sprigs, to serve

Put the fish in a food processor, or in a mortar with a pestle, and process or pound to a smooth paste. Add the onion, garlic, ginger, coriander leaves, garam masala, chilli powder and egg, and process or pound until well combined. Using wetted hands, form 1 tablespoon of the mixture into a ball. Repeat with the remaining mixture.

To make the tomato curry sauce, heat the oil in a large saucepan, add the onion, garlic and ginger, and cook, stirring frequently, over medium heat for 8 minutes, or until lightly golden.

Add the spices and cook, stirring, for 2 minutes, or until aromatic. Add the tomato and

250 ml (9 fl oz/1 cup) water, then reduce the heat and simmer, stirring frequently, for 15 minutes, or until reduced and thickened.

Meanwhile, heat the oil in a large frying pan to the depth of 2 cm (¾ in). Add the fish koftas in 3 or 4 batches and cook for 3 minutes, or until browned all over. Drain on paper towel.

Add the koftas to the sauce and simmer over low heat for 5 minutes, or until heated through. Gently fold in the coriander, season with salt and serve garnished with coriander sprigs.

SERVES 6

THAI BASIL, BEEF AND GREEN PEPPERCORN CURRY

There are two ingredients in this dish that make it distinctly Thai. The first is Thai basil, with its distinctive perfume and clean flavour. The second is pickled green peppercorns which add a salty, vinegary, slightly sweet quality, without too much heat.

2 tablespoons grated ginger

2 garlic cloves, crushed

500 g (1 lb 2 oz) rump or round steak

250 ml (9 fl oz/1 cup) coconut cream

1 tablespoon ready-made yellow curry paste or see recipe on page 39

80 ml (2½ fl oz/⅓ cup) fish sauce

60 g (2¼ oz/⅓ cup) shaved palm sugar (jaggery)

2 lemongrass stems, white part only, finely chopped

1 thick slice galangal

4 makrut (kaffir lime) leaves

2 tomatoes, cut into 2 cm (¾ in) dice

400 g (14 oz) tinned bamboo pieces, drained, cut into small chunks

25 g (1 oz) Thai pickled green peppercorns, on the stem

2 tablespoons tamarind purée

1 large handful Thai basil, chopped

Crush the ginger and garlic to a rough pulp in a mortar with a pestle, or food processor. Cut the meat into strips 5 cm x 2 m (2 in x ¾ in) and 3 mm (⅛ in) thick. Toss the ginger and garlic paste together with the beef and marinate for 30 minutes.

Bring half the coconut cream to the boil in a heavy-based casserole dish over medium heat then reduce to a simmer. Stir in the yellow curry paste and cook for 3–5 minutes. Add the fish sauce and palm sugar and stir until sugar is dissolved.

Increase heat to high, add the remaining ingredients and 375 ml (13 fl oz/1½ cups) water and bring the curry to the boil then reduce to a simmer and cook uncovered for 1–1¼ hours, or until the beef is tender.

Check seasoning and correct by adding extra fish sauce or palm sugar if necessary. Stir through the remaining coconut cream and serve immediately.

SERVES 4

Right: Pound the ginger and garlic together to a rough pulp.

Far right: Stir in the yellow curry paste and cook until aromatic.

SPICES

It is the aromas and flavours generated by the release of natural oils during the grinding process that makes a made-from-scratch spice blend, or curry paste, unique and irresistible.

Whole spices — being the dried seeds, stems, bark or roots of particular plants — are dry-fried or roasted then finely ground to a powder to release their natural, aromatic oils. The most commonly known of these spice blends is curry powder. This mixture comes in several guises, forming the flavour structure for many curries, particularly Indian and Sri Lankan varieties. Although mainly used as the base flavour for cooked dishes, some spice blends, such as garam masala or five-spice, are often utilized at the end of the cooking process as a final aromatic addition.

You will find most well-known spice blends in supermarkets but, as with curry pastes, fresh is undoubtedly best. Fresh, whole spices retain the natural oils which carry flavour and aroma. If the spices are old or have been pre-ground for some time, they may have lost flavour due to age and exposure to air. So it is best to buy small amounts of whole spices and replace them as required.

Spices should be bought in small quantities and used up quickly as they deteriorate when exposed to air. Fresh whole spices contain more essential oils than pre-ground or those that have been sitting in the cupboard for some time. Dry fry the spices in a frying pan over medium–high heat for 2–3 minutes, or until fragrant, to release the oils and make the spices more brittle for grinding. To grind the spices, allow them to cool then tip into a mortar and pound with a pestle until finely ground. The grinding releases the flavours and aromas and allows them to travel more evenly through the curry.

To make your own spice blend, first dry-fry spices. Ideally, dry-fry each spice separately to obtain optimum flavour as certain spices, depending on size and moisture content, will take longer than others to become fragrant. This process mellows the flavour of the spices, making for a well-rounded final result in your cooking. Allow the spices to cool then put them in a mortar and pound with a pestle until finely ground. You can also use a coffee or spice grinder. Store ground spices in a clean, well-sealed glass jar for up to 3 weeks, at which time the flavour will diminish rapidly.

Commercially produced curry pastes certainly have their place, but nothing will ever compete with a fresh, home-made batch.

To make your own curry paste, first ensure that in addition to the spices, any fresh produce required should be just that — fresh, as well as firm, crisp, unblemished and aromatic. Shrivelled up leafy herbs and chillies, dried up garlic, ginger and lemon grass or soft onions will result in an inferior product. To obtain the maximum flavour and aroma from your curry pastes, put the spice blend and fresh ingredients into the hollow of a mortar then pound and grind with a pestle until the mixture becomes pulpy then as smooth as possible.

FIVE-SPICE PORK CURRY

This dish draws on various influences to create a spicy, salty and fragrant dish. Five-spice is widely used in many Asian countries besides China, and here it is mixed with kecap manis, a thick, sweet, dark soy sauce from Indonesia.

500 g (1 lb 2 oz) pork spare ribs
1 ½ tablespoons oil
2 garlic cloves, crushed
190 g (6¾ oz) fried tofu puffs
1 tablespoon finely chopped ginger
1 teaspoon five-spice
½ teaspoon ground white pepper

3 tablespoons fish sauce
3 tablespoons kecap manis
2 tablespoons light soy sauce
35 g (1 ¼ oz/¼ cup) shaved palm sugar (jaggery)
1 small handful coriander (cilantro) leaves, chopped
100 g (3½ oz), snow peas (mangetout), thinly sliced

Cut the spare ribs into 2.5 cm (1 in) thick pieces, discarding any small pieces of bone. Put into a saucepan and cover with cold water. Bring to the boil then reduce to a simmer and cook for 5 minutes. Drain and set aside.

Heat the oil in a heavy-based saucepan over medium–high heat. Add the pork and garlic and stir until lightly browned. Add remaining ingredients except snow peas, plus 560 ml (19¼ fl oz/2¼ cups) water. Cover, bring to the boil then reduce to a simmer and cook, stirring occasionally, for 15–18 minutes, or until the pork is tender. Stir in the snow peas and serve.

SERVES 4

Paneer and Pea Curry

This substantial yet fragrant dish is an excellent starting point for a vegetarian meal. Paneer is an Indian cottage cheese that is made by heating and curdling milk, then separating the solids. It should always be made freshly, as it lasts only a few days.

PANEER

2 litres (70 fl oz/8 cups) milk

80 ml (2½ fl oz/⅓ cup) lemon juice

oil for deep-frying

CURRY PASTE

2 large onions

3 garlic cloves

1 teaspoon grated ginger

1 teaspoon cumin seeds

3 dried red chillies

1 teaspoon cardamom seeds

4 cloves

1 teaspoon fennel seeds

2 pieces cassia bark

500 g (1 lb 2 oz) peas

2 tablespoons oil

400 ml (14 fl oz) tomato passata (puréed tomatoes)

1 tablespoon garam masala

1 teaspoon ground coriander

¼ teaspoon ground turmeric

1 tablespoon cream (whipping)

coriander (cilantro) leaves, to serve

Put the milk in a large saucepan, bring to the boil, stir in the lemon juice and turn off the heat. Stir the mixture for 1–2 seconds as it curdles. Put in a colander and leave for 30 minutes for the whey to drain off. Place the paneer curds on a clean, flat surface, cover with a plate, weigh down and leave for at least 4 hours.

Put all the curry paste ingredients in a food processor, or in a mortar with a pestle, and process or pound to a smooth paste.

Cut the solid paneer into 2 cm (¾ in) cubes. Fill a deep heavy-based saucepan one-third full of oil and heat to 180°C (350°F), or until a cube of bread browns in 15 seconds. Cook the paneer in

batches for 2–3 minutes, or until golden. Drain on paper towel.

Bring a saucepan of water to the boil, add the peas and cook for 3 minutes, or until tender. Drain and set aside.

Heat the oil in a large saucepan, add the curry paste and cook over medium heat for 4 minutes, or until fragrant. Add the puréed tomato, spices, cream and 125 ml (4 fl oz/½ cup) water. Season with salt and simmer over medium heat for 5 minutes. Add the paneer and peas and cook for 3 minutes. Garnish with coriander leaves and serve.

SERVES 5

Kenyan Coriander Lamb

Much of Kenyan cuisine is fairly simple, so it is a surprise to come across Indian spices and Arabian and Portuguese influences in a curry. But the Swahili cuisine of the Kenyan coast is a vibrant fusion, producing colourful and richly spiced dishes.

1½ tablespoons chopped ginger
2½ tablespoons lemon juice
1 kg (2 lb 4 oz) lamb leg or shoulder, diced
1½ tablespoons coriander seeds
¼ teaspoon black peppercorns
2 tomatoes, chopped
2 teaspoons tomato paste (concentrated purée)
3 long green chillies, seeded, chopped

1 handful coriander (cilantro) stalks and roots,
  roughly chopped
3 tablespoons oil
250 ml (9 fl oz/1 cup) chicken stock
2 tablespoons plain yoghurt
1 large handful coriander (cilantro) leaves, finely chopped,
  to serve

Put the garlic, ginger, lemon juice and enough water to form a paste in a food processor, or in a mortar with a pestle, and process or pound to a smooth paste. Put the lamb into a non-metallic bowl, add the garlic paste, and mix well to combine. Cover and refrigerate for 2 hours.

Dry-fry the coriander seeds and peppercorns in a frying pan over medium–high heat for 2–3 minutes, or until fragrant. Allow to cool. Using a mortar with a pestle, or a spice grinder, crush or grind to a powder.

Put the ground spices, tomato, tomato paste, chillies and coriander stalks and roots in a food processor, or in a mortar with a pestle, and process or pound to a smooth paste.

Heat the oil in a heavy-based saucepan over medium–high heat. Brown the lamb in batches. When all the lamb is done, return to the pan with the tomato chilli paste, and the stock. Bring to the boil then reduce to a slow simmer, cover and cook for 1½ hours, remove the lid, and cook for a further 15 minutes, or until the lamb is very tender. While cooking, skim any oil that comes to the surface and discard.

Remove from the heat and gently stir through the yoghurt, garnish with chopped coriander leaves and serve.

SERVES 6

Right: Process the garlic, ginger and lemon juice until smooth.

Far right: Process the spices with the tomato and tomato paste.

Spicy Chicken and Tomato Curry

This recipe leaves barely a spice untouched! Containing spices that range from hot to sweet, sharp to gently perfumed, this is a dish where the chicken supports the flavourings, not the other way round. It is also a simple dish to prepare.

1 tablespoon oil
2 x 1.5 kg (3 lb 5 oz) chickens, jointed
1 onion, sliced
½ teaspoon ground cloves
1 teaspoon ground turmeric
2 teaspoons garam masala
3 teaspoons chilli powder
3 cardamom pods
3 garlic cloves, crushed

1 tablespoon grated ginger
1 tablespoon poppy seeds
2 teaspoons fennel seeds
250 ml (9 fl oz/1 cup) coconut milk
1 star anise
1 cinnamon stick
4 large tomatoes, roughly chopped
2 tablespoons lime juice

Heat the oil in a large frying pan over medium heat, add the chicken in batches and cook for 5–10 minutes, or until browned, then transfer to a large saucepan.

Add the onion to the frying pan and cook, stirring, for 10–12 minutes, or until golden. Stir in the ground cloves, turmeric, garam masala and chilli powder, and cook, stirring, for 1 minute, then add to the chicken.

Lightly crush the cardamom pods with the flat side of a heavy knife. Remove the seeds, discarding the pods. Put the seeds and the garlic, ginger,

poppy seeds, fennel seeds and 2 tablespoons of the coconut milk in a food processor, or in a mortar with a pestle, and process or pound to a smooth paste. Add the spice mixture, remaining coconut milk, star anise, cinnamon stick, tomato and 3 tablespoons water to the chicken.

Simmer, covered, for 45 minutes, or until the chicken is tender. Remove the chicken, cover and keep warm. Bring the cooking liquid to the boil and boil for 20–25 minutes, or until reduced by half. Put the chicken on a serving plate, mix the lime juice with the cooking liquid and pour over the chicken.

SERVES 8-10

Far left: Brown the chicken in the frying pan in batches.

Left: Fry the onions until golden before adding the spices.

Thai Green Curry with Fish Balls

A long-time Thai favourite, this dish features fish balls or dumplings rather than pieces of fish. Thai eggplants (aubergines), galangal and tangy makrut (kaffir lime) leaves add depth to the spicy curry base, while the pounded fish provides texture.

350 g (12 oz), skinless, firm white fish fillets, roughly cut into pieces
3 tablespoons coconut cream
2 tablespoons ready-made green curry paste or see recipe on page 120
440 ml (15¼ fl oz/1¾ cups) coconut milk (do not shake the tin), plus extra for topping
175 g (6 oz) Thai apple eggplants (aubergines), quartered

175 g (6 oz) pea eggplants (aubergines)
2 tablespoons fish sauce
2 tablespoons shaved palm sugar (jaggery)
50 g (1¾ oz) finely sliced galangal
3 makrut (kaffir lime) leaves, torn in half
1 handful holy basil to serve
½ long red chilli, seeded, finely sliced, to serve

Put the fish fillets in a food processor, or in a mortar with a pestle, and process or pound to a smooth paste.

Put the thick coconut cream from the top of the tin in a saucepan, bring to a rapid simmer over medium heat, stirring occasionally, and cook for 5–10 minutes, or until the mixture 'splits' (the oil starts to separate). Add the curry paste and cook for 5 minutes, or until fragrant. Add the remaining coconut milk and mix well.

Use a spoon or your wet hands to shape the fish paste into small balls, about 2 cm (¾ in) across, and drop them into the coconut milk. Add the eggplants, fish sauce and sugar and cook for 12–15 minutes, stirring occasionally, or until the fish and eggplants are cooked.

Stir in the galangal and makrut leaves. Taste, then adjust the seasoning if necessary. Spoon into a serving bowl and sprinkle with extra coconut milk, basil leaves and sliced chilli.

SERVES 4

Right: Stir the paste into the coconut cream and cook until fragrant.

Far right: Shape the fish paste into small balls with wet hands.

Prawns with Thai Basil

This fragrant curry couldn't be easier to make. Once the prawns (shrimp) are prepared, the cooking takes only minutes. The sauce should be thick, hot and sweet, so make sure your saucepan or wok is hot enough to reduce the coconut milk as soon as it is added.

CURRY PASTE
2 dried long red chillies
2 lemongrass stems, white part only, finely sliced
2.5 cm (1 in) piece galangal, finely sliced
5 garlic cloves, crushed
4 red Asian shallots, finely chopped
6 coriander (cilantro) roots, finely chopped
1 teaspoon shrimp paste
1 teaspoon ground cumin
3 tablespoons chopped unsalted peanuts

600 g (1 lb 5 oz) raw prawns (shrimp), peeled, deveined, tails intact
2 tablespoons oil
185 ml (6 fl oz/¾ cup) coconut milk
2 teaspoons fish sauce
2 teaspoons shaved palm sugar (jaggery)
1 handful Thai basil leaves, to serve

Soak the chillies in boiling water for 5 minutes, or until soft. Remove the seeds and stems and chop. Put the chillies and the remaining curry paste ingredients in a food processor, or in a mortar with a pestle, and process or pound to a smooth paste.

Cut each prawn along the back so it opens like a butterfly (leave each prawn joined along the base and at the tail).

Heat the oil in a saucepan or wok and stir-fry 2 tablespoons of the curry paste over a medium heat for 2 minutes, or until fragrant.

Add the coconut milk, fish sauce and palm sugar and cook for a few seconds. Add the prawns and cook for a few minutes or until cooked through. Taste, then adjust the seasoning if necessary. Serve garnished with Thai basil.

SERVES 4

LAMB AND SPINACH CURRY

This is a richly flavoured, traditional dish from the Punjab region of northern India. It is cooked until the sauce is very thick and fairly dry and the distinctive flavours of the lamb and English spinach have blended to form a smooth, unified whole.

2 teaspoons coriander seeds
1 ½ teaspoons cumin seeds
3 tablespoons oil
1 kg (2 lb 4 oz) boneless leg or shoulder of lamb,
    cut into 2.5 cm (1 in) cubes
4 onions, finely chopped
6 cloves
6 cardamom pods
1 cinnamon stick
10 black peppercorns

4 Indian bay (cassia) leaves
3 teaspoons garam masala
¼ teaspoon ground turmeric
1 teaspoon paprika
1 ½ tablespoons grated ginger
4 garlic cloves, crushed
185 g (6½ oz/¾ cup) Greek-style yoghurt
450 g (1 lb) amaranth or English spinach leaves,
    roughly chopped

Dry-fry the coriander and cumin seeds in a frying pan over medium–high heat for 2–3 minutes, or until fragrant. Allow to cool. Using a mortar with a pestle, or a spice grinder, crush or grind to a powder.

Heat the oil in a flameproof casserole dish over low heat and fry a few pieces of meat at a time until browned. Remove from the dish. Add more oil to the dish, if necessary, and fry the onion, cloves, cardamom pods, cinnamon stick, peppercorns and bay leaves until the onion is lightly browned. Add the cumin and coriander, garam masala, turmeric and paprika and fry for 30 seconds.

Add the meat, ginger, garlic, yoghurt and 425 ml (15 fl oz) water and bring to the boil. Reduce the heat to a simmer, cover and cook for 1½–2 hours, or until the meat is very tender. At this stage, most of the water should have evaporated. If it hasn't, remove the lid, increase the heat and cook until the moisture has evaporated.

Cook the spinach briefly in a little simmering water until it is just wilted, then refresh in cold water. Drain thoroughly, then finely chop. Squeeze out any extra water. Add the spinach to the lamb and cook for 3 minutes, or until the spinach and lamb are well mixed and any extra liquid has evaporated.

SERVES 6

Green Herb Pork Curry

A generous use of coriander (cilantro) and dill, mixed with yoghurt and added at the last minute to the curry, gives this dish a burst of fresh herb flavour. Balancing this are the warmer, rounder, roasted aromas of fennel and coriander seeds.

2 teaspoons coriander seeds
2 teaspoons fennel seeds
¼ teaspoon ground white pepper
1½ tablespoons grated ginger
6 garlic cloves, crushed
2 onions, chopped
3 tablespoons oil

1 kg (2 lb 4 oz) pork shoulder, cut into 2 cm (¾ in) dice
250 ml (9 fl oz/1 cup) chicken stock
125 g (4½ oz/½ cup) plain yoghurt
1 large handful coriander (cilantro) leaves,
    roughly chopped
1 large handful dill, roughly chopped

Dry-fry the coriander and fennel seeds in a frying pan over medium–high heat for 2–3 minutes, or until fragrant. Allow to cool. Using a mortar with a pestle, or a spice grinder, crush or grind to a powder.

Put the ground coriander and fennel seeds along with the pepper, ginger, garlic and onion in a food processor, or in a mortar with a pestle, and process or pound to a smooth paste. Add a little water if it is too thick.

Heat 2 tablespoons of the oil in a heavy-based saucepan over high heat, and brown the pork in batches. Set aside. Reduce heat to low then add

the remaining oil, and cook the spice and onion paste, stirring constantly, for 5–8 minutes. Add the pork back to the pan, and stir to coat with the paste. Add the chicken stock, increase heat to high and bring to the boil then reduce to a very slow simmer, cover and cook for 2–2½ hours, or until the pork is very tender. While cooking, stir occasionally and skim any oil that comes to the surface and discard.

Put the yoghurt, chopped coriander, dill and 3 tablespoons of the cooking liquid from the pork into a jug or bowl and blend with a stick blender until smooth, then add back into the pork. Remove from heat, season well to taste and serve.

SERVES 6

Far left: Process or pound the onion mixture to a smooth paste.

Left: Blend the yoghurt, herbs and cooking liquid until smooth.

CHICKEN MASALA

Masala simply means 'mixture of spices', a catch-all word that could be used with just about any curry. In this case, the mixture is aromatic but only moderately spicy, giving the dish a subtle flavour.

1.5 kg (3 lb 5 oz) chicken thigh fillets or chicken pieces, skinless
2 teaspoons ground cumin
2 teaspoons ground coriander
1 1/2 teaspoons garam masala
1/4 teaspoon ground turmeric
2 onions, finely chopped
4 garlic cloves, roughly chopped

5 cm (2 in) piece ginger, roughly chopped
2 ripe tomatoes, chopped
3 tablespoons ghee or oil
5 cloves
8 cardamom pods, bruised
1 cinnamon stick
10 curry leaves
160 g (5¾ oz/⅔ cup) Greek-style yoghurt

Trim off any excess fat from the chicken. Mix the cumin, coriander, garam masala and turmeric together and rub it into the chicken.

Put half the onion with the garlic, ginger and chopped tomato in a food processor, or in a mortar with a pestle, and process or pound to a smooth paste.

Heat the ghee or oil in a casserole dish over low heat, add the remaining onion, cloves, cardamom, cinnamon and curry leaves and fry until the onion is golden brown. Add the tomato and onion paste

and stir for 5 minutes. Season with salt, to taste. Add the yoghurt and whisk until smooth, then add the spiced chicken. Toss pieces through and bring slowly to the boil.

Reduce the heat, cover and simmer for 50 minutes or until the oil separates from the sauce. Stir the ingredients occasionally to prevent the chicken from sticking. If the sauce is too thin, simmer for a couple of minutes with the lid off.

SERVES 4

Chapter 5

SOFTLY SWEET

These curries may appear less traditional than others but they feature a wide range of ingredients — such as pineapple, apricots, orange juice, honey, almonds, raisins and mint — that give them a gentle sweetness. Add a sprinkle of sweet spices such as cinnamon, saffron and cardamom for a truly sweet curry.

Barbecue Duck Curry With Lychees

This colourful curry features the delicate appeal of lychees. Lychees have a creamy, sweet flesh and gentle perfume. The spice paste is earthy and peppery, rather than hot, and balances well with the rich-tasting meat and coconut.

CURRY PASTE

1 teaspoon white peppercorns

1 teaspoon shrimp paste

3 long red chillies, seeded

1 red onion, roughly chopped

2 garlic cloves

2 lemongrass stems, white part only, thinly sliced

5 cm (2 in) piece ginger

3 coriander (cilantro) roots

5 makrut (kaffir lime) leaves

2 tablespoons oil

2 teaspoons ground coriander

1 teaspoon ground cumin

1 teaspoon paprika

1 teaspoon ground turmeric

1 Chinese barbecue duck

400 ml (14 fl oz) coconut cream

1 tablespoon shaved palm sugar (jaggery)

2 tablespoons fish sauce

1 thick slice galangal

240 g (8½ oz) tinned straw mushrooms, drained

400 g (14 oz) tinned lychees, cut in half
(reserve 3 tablespoons. syrup)

250 g (9 oz) cherry tomatoes

1 handful Thai basil, chopped

1 handful coriander (cilantro) leaves, chopped

Dry-fry the peppercorns and the shrimp paste wrapped in some foil in a frying pan over medium–high heat for 2–3 minutes, or until fragrant. Allow to cool. Using a mortar with a pestle, or a spice grinder, crush or grind the peppercorns to a powder. Put the crushed peppercorns and the shrimp with the remaining curry paste ingredients in a food processor, or in a mortar with a pestle, and process or pound to a smooth paste.

Remove the duck meat from the bones and chop into bite-sized pieces. Put the thick coconut cream from the top of the tin in a saucepan, bring to a rapid simmer over medium heat, stirring occasionally, and cook for 5–10 minutes, or until

the mixture 'splits' (the oil starts to separate). Add half the curry paste, palm sugar and fish sauce and stir until the palm sugar is dissolved. Add the duck, galangal, straw mushrooms, lychees, reserved lychee syrup and remaining coconut cream. Bring to the boil then reduce to a simmer and cook for 15–20 minutes, or until the duck is tender.

Add the cherry tomatoes, basil and coriander. Season to taste. Serve when the cherry tomatoes are slightly softened.

Note: When in season, you can use fresh lychees, which will be sweeter and juicier than the tinned variety so you won't need the added syrup.

SERVES 4

CHICKEN, ALMOND AND RAISIN CURRY

While the chicken cooks, you will be able to savour the wonderful aromas coming from this sweetly spiced curry. The spices are in perfect harmony with each other: cloves and ginger provide sharpness, while the almonds and raisins add a touch of luxury.

6 cardamom pods
6 cloves
1 teaspoon cumin seeds
½ teaspoon cayenne pepper
2 tablespoons ghee or oil
1 kg (2 lb 4 oz) chicken thigh fillets, cut into 3 cm (1¼ in) cubes
1 onion, finely chopped

3 garlic cloves, crushed
1½ tablespoons finely grated ginger
2 cinnamon sticks
2 bay leaves
50 g (1¾ oz/⅓ cup), blanched almonds, lightly toasted
40 g (1½ oz/⅓ cup) raisins
250 g (9 oz/1 cup) plain yoghurt
125 ml (4 fl oz/½ cup) chicken stock

Lightly crush the cardamom pods with the flat side of a heavy knife. Remove the seeds, discarding the pods. Dry-fry the seeds along with the cloves, cumin seeds and cayenne pepper in a frying pan over medium–high heat for 2–3 minutes, or until fragrant. Allow to cool. Using a mortar with a pestle, or a spice grinder, crush or grind to a powder.

In a large heavy-based frying pan, heat the ghee or oil over medium–high heat. Brown the chicken in batches and set aside. In the same pan, cook the onion, garlic and ginger over low heat for 5–8 minutes until softened. Add the ground spice mix, cinnamon sticks and bay leaves, and cook, stirring constantly, for 5 minutes. Put the almonds, raisins and chicken back into the pan. Add the yoghurt a spoonful at a time, stirring to incorporate it into the dish. Add the chicken stock, reduce the heat to low, cover and cook for 40 minutes, or until the chicken is tender. While cooking, skim any oil that comes to the surface and discard. Season well and serve.

SERVES 6

Indian Pork, Honey and Almond Curry

This unusual curry blends aromatic cinnamon and cardamom with sweet honey and almonds, fragrant citrus and the fresh parsley and coriander (cilantro). Pork is the perfect complement for this mix of aromas and flavours.

1 cinnamon stick
3 cardamom pods
750 g (1 lb 10 oz) boneless pork shoulder
1 tablespoon oil
2 tablespoons honey
3 garlic cloves, crushed
2 onions, chopped
150 ml (5 fl oz) chicken stock

1 teaspoon ground turmeric
½ teaspoon ground black pepper
1 teaspoon grated lemon zest
1 teaspoon grated orange zest
250 g (9 oz/1 cup) plain yoghurt
30 g (1 oz/¼ cup) slivered almonds, toasted
1 small handful coriander (cilantro) leaves, chopped
1 small handful flat-leaf (Italian) parsley, chopped

Dry-fry the cinnamon and cardamom in a frying pan over medium–high heat for 2–3 minutes, or until fragrant. Allow to cool. Using a mortar with a pestle, or a spice grinder, crush or grind to a powder.

Cut the pork into 2 cm (¾ in) cubes. Heat the oil and honey in a heavy-based saucepan over medium heat. Add the cubed pork, garlic and onion and cook for 8–10 minutes, or until onion is translucent and pork light golden. Add 200 ml (7 fl oz) water and the chicken stock,

bring to the boil then reduce to a simmer, cover and cook, stirring occasionally, for 1 hour 15 minutes, or until the pork is tender.

Uncover and bring to a rapid simmer for 10 minutes, or until most of the liquid is absorbed. Add the crushed spices, turmeric, pepper, 1 teaspoon salt and the citrus zest and simmer for a further 3–4 minutes. To serve, gently reheat, stirring in the yoghurt, almonds, chopped coriander and flat-leaf parsley.

SERVES 4

Far left: Cut the boneless pork shoulder fillet into neat cubes.

Left: Stir in the spices, salt and grated citrus zest and simmer.

Indonesian Pumpkin and Spinach Curry

This curry contains some of the classic ingredients of Indonesian cooking, including candlenuts, shallots, galangal and sambal oelek. Sambal means hot and spicy — which gives you an idea of the dish's taste.

CURRY PASTE
3 candlenuts
1 tablespoon raw peanuts
3 red Asian shallots, chopped
2 garlic cloves
2–3 teaspoons sambal oelek
1/4 teaspoon ground turmeric
1 teaspoon grated galangal

2 tablespoons oil
1 onion, finely chopped
600 g (1 lb 5 oz) butternut pumpkin (squash), cut into
    2 cm (3/4 in) cubes
125 ml (4 fl oz/1/2 cup) vegetable stock (or as required)
350 g (12 oz) English spinach, roughly chopped
400 ml (14 fl oz) coconut cream
1/4 teaspoon sugar

Put all the curry paste ingredients in a food processor, or in a mortar with a pestle, and process or pound to a smooth paste.

Heat the oil in a large saucepan, add the curry paste and cook, stirring, over low heat for 3–5 minutes, or until fragrant. Add the onion and cook for a further 5 minutes, or until softened.

Add the pumpkin and half the vegetable stock and cook, covered, for 10 minutes, or until pumpkin is almost cooked through. Add more stock, if required. Add the spinach, coconut cream and sugar, and season with salt. Bring to the boil, stirring constantly, then reduce the heat and simmer for 3–5 minutes, or until the spinach is cooked and the sauce has thickened slightly. Serve immediately.

SERVES 6

Right: Process all the paste ingredients to form a smooth paste.

Far right: Add the pumpkin with the stock and cook until almost tender.

Minced Lamb with Orange

There is probably no meat more versatile than lamb. This non-traditional curry blends aromatic ground spices with the sweetness of orange juice and the cleansing freshness of green chillies and mint. It is a thick, wet curry — ideal for serving with bread.

3 tablespoons oil
2 onions, finely diced
4 garlic cloves, crushed
3 teaspoons finely grated ginger
2 teaspoons ground cumin
2 teaspoons ground coriander
1/2 teaspoon ground turmeric
1/2 teaspoon cayenne pepper
1 teaspoon garam masala

1 kg (2 lb 4 oz) minced (ground) lamb
90 g (3 1/4 oz/ 1/3 cup) plain yoghurt
250 ml (9 fl oz/1 cup) orange juice
2 teaspoons orange zest
1 bay leaf
1 long green chilli, seeded, finely sliced
1 handful coriander (cilantro) leaves, roughly chopped
1 handful mint, roughly chopped

Heat the oil in a large heavy-based frying pan over medium heat. Add the onions, garlic, and ginger and sauté for 5 minutes. Add the cumin, coriander, turmeric, cayenne pepper and garam masala, and cook for a further 5 minutes.

Increase the heat to high, add the lamb mince, and cook, stirring constantly to break the meat up. Add the yoghurt, a tablespoon at a time, stirring so that it combines well. Add the orange juice, zest, and bay leaf.

Bring to the boil then reduce to a simmer, cover and cook for 45 minutes, or until tender. While cooking, skim any oil that comes to the surface and discard. Season well to taste then stir through the green chilli, coriander and mint before serving.

SERVES 6

SNAPPER WITH GREEN BANANAS AND MANGO

This impressive-looking curry is richly flavoured with spices, herbs and tropical fruit. Fruit like green banana makes an interesting textural addition to curries — the banana is very starchy, more like a vegetable than a fruit, and will help to thicken the curry.

CURRY PASTE

3 teaspoons coriander seeds
1 teaspoon cumin seeds
2–3 dried long red chillies
2 lemongrass stems, white part only, finely sliced
3 red Asian shallots, finely chopped
2 garlic cloves, crushed
1 teaspoon ground turmeric
1 teaspoon shrimp paste

1 teaspoon ground turmeric
1 small green banana or plantain, thinly sliced
3 tablespoons coconut cream
1 tablespoon fish sauce
1 teaspoon shaved palm sugar (jaggery)
400 g (14 oz) snapper or other skinless, firm white fish fillets, cut into large cubes
315 ml (10¾ fl oz/1¼ cups) coconut milk
1 small mango, just ripe, cut into thin slices
1 long green chilli, finely sliced
12 Thai basil leaves

Dry-fry the coriander and cumin seeds in a frying pan over medium–high heat for 2–3 minutes, or until fragrant. Allow to cool. Using a mortar with a pestle, or a spice grinder, crush or grind to a powder.

Soak the chillies in boiling water for 5 minutes, or until soft. Remove the stem and seeds, then chop. Put the chillies, the ground coriander and cumin seeds with the remaining curry paste ingredients in a food processor, or in a mortar with a pestle, and process or pound to a smooth paste. Add a little oil if it is too thick.

Bring a small saucepan of water to the boil. Add 1 teaspoon salt, turmeric and banana slices and simmer for 10 minutes, then drain.

Put the coconut cream in a saucepan, bring to a rapid simmer over medium heat, stirring occasionally, and cook for 5–10 minutes, or until the mixture 'splits' (the oil starts to separate). Add 2 tablespoons of the made curry paste, stir well to combine and cook until fragrant. Add the fish sauce and sugar and cook for another 2 minutes or until the mixture begins to darken.

Add the fish pieces and stir well to coat the fish in the curry mixture. Slowly add the coconut milk until it has all been incorporated.

Add the banana, mango, green chilli and the basil leaves to the pan and gently stir to combine all the ingredients. Cook for a further 1–2 minutes, then serve.

SERVES 4

Minted Lamb Curry

Fresh tasting, mint is more often associated with chutneys, salads and teas than curries, but this simple dish proves that it can work well in this arena, too. Here, it is combined with coriander (cilantro), green chillies and lemon juice, creating a refreshing curry.

1 kg (2 lb 4 oz) lamb shoulder, cut into 2 cm (³/₄ in) dice
4 onions, finely sliced
3 garlic cloves, crushed
3 teaspoons finely chopped ginger
½ teaspoon cayenne pepper
1 teaspoon turmeric

125 ml (4 fl oz/½ cup) chicken stock
1 handful coriander (cilantro) leaves and stalks
1 handful mint
3 long green chillies
3 tablespoons lemon juice
1 teaspoon sugar

Put the lamb, onions, garlic, ginger, cayenne, turmeric, and chicken stock in a heavy-based saucepan over medium heat. Bring to a simmer, reduce to low heat, cover and cook for 2 hours. Skim the surface to remove any oil and discard.

Put the coriander leaves and stalks, mint leaves, green chillies, lemon juice and 2 tablespoons of cooking liquid from the curry in a food processor, or in a mortar with a pestle, and process or pound to a smooth consistency. Pour into the lamb mixture, put back on the heat until it just comes back up to a simmer. Add the sugar, season well to taste and serve.

SERVES 6

RICE

◇◇◇◇◇◇◇◇◇◇◇◇◇◇◇◇◇◇◇◇◇◇◇◇◇◇◇◇◇◇◇◇◇◇◇◇◇◇

Anywhere there is curry,
rice will be close to hand.

In places such as China, Japan and Korea, where chopsticks are used, medium or short-grain rices, which tend to stick together, are preferred. In India, Sri Lanka and Malaysia, a rice that cooks into separate fluffy grains is more sought after. The Vietnamese eat both glutinous (sticky) rice and fluffy, dry rice. In Thailand, long-grain jasmine rice is eaten, with the exception of some parts of the north where glutinous rice is preferred.

There are more than 2000 types of rice. Mostly, rice is classified by the shape, or size, of the grain. However, texture, fragrance and colour also distinguish one type from another.

Although there are three basic rice types available, only long-grain is considered the natural accompaniment to curries. Compared with short- and medium-grain rices, long-grain is generally thinner, longer, less starchy and when cooked yields a light fluffy, loose-grained texture. There are several varieties of long-grain rice and although, at a pinch, any will do the trick, for authenticity try serving the dry, separate grained, nutty-tasting basmati rice with Indian curries and aromatic, slightly clingy, floral scented jasmine rice alongside Thai curries. The flavours of both these rice varieties complement the spices in the curries from the corresponding cuisines.

There are two main ways of cooking rice.

ABSORPTION METHOD
Put the rice in a saucepan and shake so that it evenly coats the bottom of the pan. Stick the very tip of your finger into the rice then add enough cold water to come up to the first finger joint. Bring to the boil over high heat then cover with a clear, tight-fitting lid. Reduce heat to low and cook until the water has mostly evaporated and small steam holes appear on the surface of the rice. Remove the lid, fluff with a fork and serve.

RAPID BOIL METHOD
Bring a large saucepan of water to the boil over high heat. Sprinkle over the rice and cook according to the instructions on the packet or until the grains are tender. Drain the rice in a colander. If using jasmine rice, which is slightly glutinous, rinse with a little tepid water before serving.

Once you have opened a packet of rice, store it in a cool, dry place in an airtight container. Rice bought in large sacks is best stored in a dry, clean container with a lid. An unopened packet will keep for up to a year. Brown rice still contains the oil-rich germ or bran layer, so it will turn rancid if left in a warm place for too long; store it in an airtight container in the refrigerator. You also need to take extra care with cooked rice. If it is not consumed immediately, cover it, then chill it quickly as harmful bacteria can grow rapidly. Cooked rice will store in the refrigerator for up to 2 days.

LAMB RIZALA

Traditionally, rizala featured mutton, so slow cooking was the ideal method, but this applies equally to lamb shoulder. The yoghurt further tenderizes the meat, helping it absorb the aromatics, creating melt-in-the-mouth tender, flavoursome meat.

2 onions, chopped
1 tablespoon grated ginger
4 garlic cloves, crushed
1 teaspoon ground cinnamon
3 tablespoons ghee or oil
1 kg (2 lb 4 oz) lamb shoulder, diced

125 g (4½ oz/½ cup) plain yoghurt
250 ml (9 fl oz/1 cup) chicken stock
40 g (1½ oz/½ cup) crisp fried onion
3 red chillies, seeded, finely sliced
1 tablespoon sugar
3 tablespoons lime juice

Put the onions, ginger, garlic, cinnamon and 3 tablespoons of water in a food processor, or in a mortar with a pestle, and process or pound to a smooth paste.

Heat the ghee or oil in a heavy-based saucepan over high heat. Brown the lamb in batches and set aside.

Reduce the heat to low, add the onion paste and cook for 5 minutes, stirring constantly. Put the lamb back into the pan, and stir to combine, add the yoghurt a spoon at a time, stirring well to incorporate. Add the chicken stock, and crisp fried onion. Bring to a simmer, cover and cook over low heat for 2 hours. While cooking, skim any oil that comes to the surface and discard.

When the lamb is tender, add the chillies, sugar and lime juice, and cook for 5 minutes more before serving.

SERVES 6

VIETNAMESE MILD CHICKEN CURRY

Vietnamese food is a mix of indigenous, French and Asian influences. Curries are found mainly in the tropical southern areas of the country, and though often showing links with Indian cooking, are not as rich or as spicy as those from India or Thailand.

4 large chicken leg quarters
1 tablespoon Indian curry powder
1 teaspoon caster (superfine) sugar
80 ml (2½ fl oz/⅓ cup) oil
500 g (1 lb 2 oz) sweet potato, cut into 3 cm (1¼ in) cubes
1 large onion, cut into thin wedges

4 garlic cloves, crushed
1 lemongrass stem, white part only, finely chopped
2 bay leaves
1 large carrot, cut into 1 cm (½ in) pieces on the diagonal
400 ml (14 fl oz) coconut milk
Thai basil, to serve

Remove the skin and any excess fat from the chicken. Pat dry with paper towel and cut each quarter into 3 even pieces. Put the curry powder, sugar, ½ teaspoon black pepper and 2 teaspoons salt in a bowl, and mix well. Rub the curry mixture into the chicken pieces. Put the chicken pieces on a plate, cover with plastic wrap and refrigerate overnight.

Heat the oil in a large saucepan. Add the sweet potato and cook over medium heat for 3 minutes, or until lightly golden. Remove with a slotted spoon.

Remove all but 2 tablespoons of the oil from the pan. Add the onion and cook, stirring, for

5 minutes. Add the garlic, lemongrass and bay leaves, and cook for 2 minutes.

Add the chicken and cook, stirring, over medium heat for 5 minutes, or until well coated in the mixture and starting to change colour. Add 250 ml (9 fl oz/1 cup) water and simmer, covered, stirring occasionally, for 20 minutes.

Stir in the carrot, sweet potato and coconut milk, and simmer, uncovered, stirring occasionally, for 30 minutes, or until the chicken is cooked and tender. Be careful not to break up the sweet potato cubes. Serve topped with Thai basil.

SERVES 6

Far left: Remove the skin and any excess fat from the chicken.

Left: Pour in the coconut milk and simmer until the chicken is tender.

Thai Sweet Pork and Pineapple Curry

This refreshing curry is a vibrant mix of fresh ingredients — pineapple, tomatoes, cucumber and coriander (cilantro) — and sweet–sour seasonings such as vinegar and palm sugar. It is a great summer dish with a refreshing, slightly spicy and sweet flavour.

500 g (1 lb 2 oz) boneless pork leg, trimmed of excess fat
1 tablespoon oil
3 garlic cloves, crushed
125 ml (4 fl oz/½ cup) brown malt vinegar
45 g (1½ oz/¼ cup) palm sugar (jaggery), shaved
3 tablespoons tomato paste (concentrated purée)
1 tomato, cut into wedges
1 onion, cut into thin wedges

90 g (3¼ oz/½ cup) pineapple, cut into chunks
½ telegraph (long) cucumber, halved lengthways, seeded, sliced
½ red capsicum (pepper), cut into strips
2½ tablespoons chopped jalapeno chillies (in brine)
2 spring onions (scallions), cut into 5 cm (2 in) pieces
1 small handful coriander (cilantro) leaves

Cut the pork into 3 cm (1¼ in) cubes. Heat the oil in a large saucepan over medium heat. Add the pork and garlic and cook for 4–5 minutes, or until pork is lightly browned.

In another saucepan, stir the vinegar, palm sugar, ½ teaspoon salt and the tomato paste over medium heat for 3 minutes, or until the palm sugar is dissolved.

Add the vinegar mixture to the pork along with the tomato, onion, pineapple, cucumber, capsicum, and jalapeños. Bring to the boil then reduce to a simmer and cook for 8–10 minutes, or until the pork is tender. Stir in the spring onions and coriander and serve.

SERVES 4

Right: Trim the pork fillet of excess fat and cut into neat cubes.

Far right: Add the cucumber and capsicum to the saucepan.

CHICKEN CURRY WITH APRICOTS

This dish is a lovely blend of sweet, rich apricots and mellow, round spices such as cumin, turmeric and cardamom. With fresh ginger and green chillies providing a bit of bite, the chicken itself seems like an almost incidental ingredient!

18 dried apricots
1 tablespoon ghee or oil
2 x 1.5 kg (3 lb 5 oz) chickens, jointed
3 onions, finely sliced
1 teaspoon grated ginger
3 garlic cloves, crushed

3 long green chillies, seeded, finely chopped
1 teaspoon cumin seeds
1 teaspoon chilli powder
1/2 teaspoon ground turmeric
4 cardamom pods, bruised
4 large tomatoes, peeled, cut into 8 pieces

Soak the dried apricots in 250 ml (9 fl oz/1 cup) hot water for 1 hour.

Melt the ghee or add the oil to a large saucepan, add the chicken in batches and cook over high heat for 5–6 minutes, or until browned. Remove from the pan. Add the onion and cook, stirring often, for 10 minutes, or until the onion has softened and turned golden brown.

Add the ginger, garlic and chopped green chilli, and cook, stirring, for 2 minutes. Stir in the cumin seeds, chilli powder and ground turmeric, and cook for a further 1 minute.

Return the chicken to the pan, add the cardamom, tomato and apricots, with any remaining liquid, and mix well. Simmer, covered, for 35 minutes, or until the chicken is tender.

Remove the chicken, cover and keep warm. Bring the liquid to the boil and boil rapidly, uncovered, for 5 minutes, or until it has thickened slightly. To serve, spoon the liquid over the chicken.

SERVES 4-6

Right: Sauté the chicken pieces in batches until browned.

Far right: Stir the spices into the onion mixture and cook until fragrant.

Thai Beef and Pumpkin Curry

Curries are as much about aroma as they are about taste, but this curry also contributes a wonderful tender texture to the mix. Soft, sweet pumpkin, rich beef and crunchy peanuts come together in a sauce that is hot, rich and sweet.

2 tablespoons oil
750 g (1 lb 10 oz) blade steak, thinly sliced
4 tablespoons ready-made Massaman curry paste or see recipe on page 19
2 garlic cloves, crushed
1 onion, sliced
6 curry leaves, torn

750 ml (26 fl oz/3 cups) coconut milk
450 g (1 lb) butternut pumpkin (squash), roughly diced
2 tablespoons chopped raw peanuts
1 tablespoon shaved palm sugar (jaggery)
2 tablespoons tamarind purée
2 tablespoons fish sauce
curry leaves, to serve

Heat a wok or frying pan over high heat. Add the oil and swirl to coat the sides. Add the meat in batches and cook for 5 minutes, or until browned. Remove the meat from the wok.

Add the curry paste, garlic, onion and curry leaves to the wok, and stir to coat. Return the meat to the wok and cook, stirring, over medium heat for 2 minutes.

Add the coconut milk to the wok, then reduce the heat and simmer for 45 minutes. Add the diced pumpkin and simmer for 25–30 minutes, or until the meat and the pumpkin are tender and the sauce has thickened.

Stir in the peanuts, palm sugar, tamarind purée and fish sauce, and simmer for 1 minute. Garnish with curry leaves and serve.

SERVES 6

Far left: Pour the coconut milk into the curry mixture and simmer.

Left: Add the pumpkin and simmer until tender and sauce thickens.

Chiang Mai Pork Curry

This Burmese-style curry is typical of the Chiang Mai area in Thailand's north. It is unlike the majority of fragrant Thai curries, in that it has a spicier, almost Indian flavour. Occasionally made with chicken, this curry improves if made in advance.

CHIANG MAI CURRY PASTE
1 tablespoon coriander seeds
2 teaspoons cumin seeds
2 dried long red chillies
1/2 teaspoon salt
5 cm (2 in) piece galangal, grated
1 lemongrass stem, white part only, finely chopped
2 red Asian shallots, chopped
2 garlic cloves, crushed
1/4 teaspoon ground turmeric
1 teaspoon shrimp paste
1/2 teaspoon ground cinnamon

500 g (1 lb 2 oz) pork belly, cut into cubes
2 tablespoons oil
2 garlic cloves, crushed
4 red Asian shallots, crushed
3 teaspoons grated ginger
4 tablespoons unsalted roasted peanuts
3 tablespoons tamarind purée
2 tablespoons fish sauce
2 tablespoons shaved palm sugar (jaggery)

Dry-fry the coriander and cumin seeds in a frying pan over medium–high heat for 2–3 minutes, or until fragrant. Allow to cool. Using a mortar with a pestle, or a spice grinder, crush or grind to a powder.

Soak the chillies in boiling water for 5 minutes, or until soft. Remove the stem and seeds, then chop. Put the chillies, the ground coriander and cumin seeds with the remaining curry paste ingredients in a food processor, or in a mortar with a pestle, and process or pound to a smooth paste. Add a little oil if it is too thick.

Blanch the pork cubes in boiling water for 1 minute, then drain well. Heat the oil in a wok or saucepan and fry the garlic for 1 minute. Add 2 tablespoons of the made curry paste and stir-fry until fragrant. Add the pork, shallots, ginger and peanuts and stir briefly. Add 500 ml (17 fl oz/2 cups) water and the tamarind purée and bring to the boil.

Add the fish sauce and sugar and simmer for 1 hour 15 minutes, or until the pork is very tender. Add more water as the pork cooks, if necessary.

SERVES 6

Chapter 5

BASICS

Once you have made a curry, serve it with an authentic and delcious
accompaniment. These are the basic breads, rice dishes and chutneys
which no cook should be without.

Saffron Rice

Saffron is the orange-red stigma of one species of the crocus plant, and the most expensive spice in the world. Its flavour is pungent and aromatic; its colour intense. It is used to flavour Indian and Persian rice dishes, such as pilaff and biryani.

400 g (14 oz/2 cups) basmati rice
25 g (1 oz) butter
3 bay leaves

¼ teaspoon saffron threads
500 ml (17 fl oz/2 cups) boiling vegetable stock

Wash rice, cover with cold water and soak for 30 minutes, then drain. Melt butter in a frying pan over medium heat, then add bay leaves and the drained rice. Cook, stirring, for 6 minutes, or until all the moisture has evaporated. Meanwhile, soak saffron threads in 2 tablespoons hot water for a few minutes then add to the rice with boiling vegetable stock, 375 ml (13 fl oz/1½ cups) boiling water and salt to taste. Bring to the boil, then reduce the heat and cook, covered, for 12–15 minutes, or until all the water is absorbed and the rice is cooked.

SERVES 6

Coconut Rice

Coconut milk is not the liquid that is found inside the coconut, which is the juice or water, but is made by soaking the grated coconut flesh in water and then squeezing it. The first soaking and squeezing gives a thicker milk, sometimes called cream.

400 g (14 oz/2 cups) long-grain rice
1 pandanus leaf

185 ml (6 fl oz/¾ cup) coconut cream

Rinse rice and cover with 1 litre (35 fl oz/4 cups) water. Set aside for 30 minutes, then drain. Bring 750 ml (26 fl oz/3 cups) water to the boil. Add the rice, pandanus leaf tied in a knot and salt to taste. Reduce the heat and cook, covered, for 12 minutes, or until the rice is just cooked. Remove from heat and add coconut cream. Stir gently to avoid breaking the grains. Cover and set aside for 10 minutes, or until the rice absorbs the coconut cream in the residual heat. Discard the pandanus leaf before serving.

SERVES 6

NAAN

Perhaps the most famous leavened bread from north India, traditionally this bread is cooked on the walls of a tandoor (clay oven). It is not easy to recreate the intense heat in a domestic oven so the texture is slightly different.

500 g (1 lb 2 oz/4 cups) plain (all-purpose) flour
1 teaspoon baking powder
½ teaspoon bicarbonate of soda (baking soda)
1 teaspoon salt
1 beaten egg

1 tablespoon melted ghee or butter
125 g (4½ oz/½ cup) plain yoghurt
250 ml (9 fl oz/1 cup) milk
6 garlic cloves (optional, for garlic naan)

Preheat the oven to 200°C (400°F/Gas 6). Lightly grease two 28 x 32 cm (11¼ x 12¾ in) baking trays.

Sift together flour, baking powder, bicarbonate of soda and salt. Mix in egg, melted ghee or butter, yoghurt and gradually add enough milk to form a soft dough. Cover with a damp cloth and leave in a warm place for 2 hours.

Knead the dough on a well-floured surface for 2–3 minutes, or until smooth. Divide into 8 portions and roll each one into an oval 15 cm (6 in) long. Brush with water and place, wet side down, on the prepared baking trays.

Brush with melted ghee or butter and bake for 8–10 minutes, or until golden brown. To make garlic naan, crush 6 garlic cloves and sprinkle evenly over the dough prior to baking.

MAKES 8

CHAPATI

Atta is made from finely ground whole durum wheat. Atta is much finer and softer than wholemeal flour so, if you can't find it, use half wholemeal and half maida or plain (all-purpose) flour instead.

280 g (10 oz/2¼ cups) atta (chapati) flour

Put flour in a large bowl with a pinch of salt. Slowly add 250 ml (9 fl oz/1 cup) water, or enough to form a firm dough. Put on a lightly floured surface and knead until smooth. Cover with plastic wrap and leave for 50 minutes. Divide into 14 portions and roll into

14 cm (5½ in) circles. Heat a frying pan over medium heat and brush with melted ghee or oil. Cook the chapatis one at a time, flattening the surface, for 2–3 minutes on each side, or until golden brown and bubbles.

MAKES 14

Roti

Roti is the generic name for bread or bread-like accompaniments. There is a great variety and they are baked, grilled (broiled), roasted or fried.

375 g (13 oz/3 cups) roti or plain (all-purpose) flour
1 teaspoon salt

2 tablespoons softened ghee

Sift flour into a large mixing bowl with salt. Rub in ghee or oil with your fingertips. Add egg and 250 ml (9 fl oz/1 cup) warm water, and mix together with a flat-bladed knife to form a moist dough.

Turn out on to a well-floured surface and knead for 10 minutes, or until you have a soft dough. Sprinkle with more flour as necessary. Form the dough into a ball and brush with oil. Place in a bowl, cover and rest for 2 hours.

Working on a lightly-floured bench top, divide the dough into 12 pieces and roll into even-sized balls. Take one ball and, working with a little oil on your fingertips, hold the ball in the air and work around the edge pulling out the dough until a 2 mm x 15 cm (1/16 x 6 in) round is formed.

Lay on a lightly-floured surface and cover with plastic wrap so that it doesn't dry out. Repeat the process with the remaining balls.

Heat a large frying pan over high heat and brush it with ghee or oil. Carefully place one roti in the frying pan, brush with some extra beaten egg and cook for 1 minute, or until the underside is golden.

Slide onto a plate and brush the pan with some more ghee or oil. Cook the other side of the roti for 50–60 seconds, or until golden. Remove from the pan and cover to keep warm. Cook the remaining rotis in the same way.

MAKES 12

Yoghurt

625 ml (22 fl oz/2½ cups) milk

2 tablespoons thick plain yoghurt

Put the milk in a heavy-based saucepan. Bring to the boil, then cool to lukewarm. Stir in the yoghurt, cover and leave in a warm place for about 8 hours, or overnight. The yoghurt should be thick. If it is too runny, the milk was probably too hot for the starter yoghurt; if it is too milky, the yoghurt was probably not left in a warm enough place to ferment.

From each batch, use 2 tablespoons to make the next batch.

When the yoghurt is set, put it in a sieve lined with a piece of muslin (cheesecloth) and leave to drain overnight. This will give a thick yoghurt that does not contain too much moisture.

PICTURE ON OPPOSITE PAGE

MAKES 625 ML (22 FL OZ/2½ CUPS)

Fresh Coconut Chutney

The coconut palm grows all over Asia and such is the importance of the fruit that it is known as shrifal, or 'fruit of lustre'. Coconut sides and drinks can either soothe and refresh palates, or add a little extra spiciness to the main event.

1 teaspoon chana dal (gram lentils)
1 teaspoon urad dal (black lentils)
grated flesh from 1/2 fresh coconut
2 green chillies, seeded, chopped
1/2 teaspoon salt

1 tablespoon oil
1 teaspoon black mustard seeds
5 curry leaves
1 teaspoon tamarind purée

Soak chana dal and urad dal in cold water for 2 hours, then drain well.

Put the flesh from the coconut, green chillies and salt in a food processor, or in a mortar with a pestle, and process or pound to a smooth paste.

Heat oil in a small saucepan and add mustard seeds and the dals, then cover and shake the pan until they pop. Add curry leaves and fry for 1 minute, or until the dal browns. Add to the coconut mixture with tamarind purée and mix well.

SERVES 4

Coconut and Coriander Chutney

90 g (3 1/4 oz) roughly chopped coriander (cilantro), including the roots
25 g (1 oz/1/4 cup) desiccated coconut
1 tablespoon soft brown sugar
1 tablespoon grated ginger

1 small onion, chopped
2 tablespoons lemon juice
1–2 green chillies, seeded
1 teaspoon salt

Put coriander, desiccated coconut, sugar, ginger, onion, lemon juice, chillies and salt in a food processor and process for 1 minute, or until finely chopped. Refrigerate until ready to serve.

There are numerous variations, depending on region and tastes. Try substituting 1 handful of

roughly chopped mint leaves for the coriander in this recipe, or add 5 roughly chopped spring onions (scallions), including the green part, instead of the onion.

If you prefer more fire in your chutney, do not remove the seeds from the chillies.

SERVES 4

Indian Tomato Oil Pickle

A juicy burst of ripe tomato on the palate can be just the thing when eating a curry. Sweet, cleansing and refreshing, it is an ideal ingredient for a relish.

2 teaspoons black or brown mustard seeds
80 ml (2½ fl oz/⅓ cup) cider vinegar, plus
    1 tablespoon extra
1 tablespoon grated ginger
5 garlic cloves, chopped
3 tablespoons oil
3 teaspoons ground cumin

2 teaspoons ground turmeric
1 teaspoon chilli powder
1 kg (2 lb 4 oz) firm, ripe tomatoes, peeled, seeded
    and chopped
3 tablespoons sugar
1 teaspoon salt
1 extra tablespoon of cider vinegar

Put mustard seeds and cider vinegar in a small saucepan, and heat over low heat for 12 minutes, or until the seeds just start to pop. The vinegar will be nearly evaporated. Allow to cool.

Put the seeds, ginger and garlic cloves in a food processor, or in a mortar with a pestle, and process or pound to a smooth paste. Heat oil in a saucepan, add cumin and turmeric and cook, stirring gently, over low heat for 4 minutes, or until fragrant. Add the mustard seed mixture, chilli powder, tomatoes, sugar and salt.

Reduce the heat and simmer, stirring occasionally, for 45 minutes, or until thick. Stir through extra cider vinegar.

Spoon into clean, warm jars, seal and cool. Refrigerate for up to 1 month.

SERVES 6

Cucumber and Tomato Raita

450 g (1 lb) grated cucumber
1 large ripe tomato, finely chopped
310 g (11 oz/1¼ cups) Greek-style yoghurt

½ tablespoon oil
1 teaspoon black mustard seeds
chopped coriander (cilantro) leaves, to serve

Put cucumber and tomato in a sieve for 20 minutes to drain off any excess liquid. Mix them in a bowl with yoghurt and season to taste with salt.

Heat oil in a small saucepan over medium heat, add mustard seeds then cover and shake the pan until the seeds start to pop. Pour the seeds and oil over the yoghurt. Serve sprinkled with coriander leaves.

SERVES 4

GLOSSARY

ALMONDS
Fragrant and creamy, almonds are used in Indian drinks and desserts, including the famous kulfi, and coconut- or yoghurt-based curries. Almonds are available whole with skins on or blanched; chopped or slivered; flaked; and ground. Use only blanched nuts in curries: to blanch, pour boiling water over and stand for 2 minutes. Drain and slip off the skins. To toast, spread the nuts on a baking tray and cook at 180°C (350°F/Gas 4) for 8–10 minutes.

BASIL
There are three main types of basil used in Thai cuisine. The most important by far is Thai basil, also known as Thai sweet basil. This variety has purplish stems, lush, deep green leaves and an aniseed aroma and flavour. It is added liberally to a wide range of dishes. The second, Holy basil, is available in two types: red- and white-stemmed. Highly perfumed and with a peppery taste, it is always cooked to release its flavour. The final type is lemon basil, also called mint basil. As its name suggests, it has a fresh, tangy scent and flavour.

CARDAMOM
Warm and pungent, with lemony undertones, cardamom has been chewed as a breath freshener from the time of the ancient Egyptians to today. Many varieties of cardamom are grown, but the smooth green pods from their native southern India and Sri Lanka are considered the best. Also of note are the large, wrinkled black (brown) pods, which have a coarser flavour. Green cardamom is difficult to harvest, making it expensive and highly valued. Both black and green cardamom are essential components of garam masala. Green cardamom is sometimes bleached to form white cardamom.

CHILLIES
There are thousands of varieties of chilli plants, with pods in an assortment of shapes, sizes and colours, and varying in their degree of hotness from gentle to positively painful. But chillies are not merely hot; each has its own flavour, and dried and fresh chillies also taste very different. Some popular varieties used in curries include cayenne, kashmiri and bird's eye chillies.

CINNAMON
Cinnamon is familiar to us all as quills of delicate, tightly rolled, light brown layers of paper-thin bark. It is indigenous to Sri Lanka, and the world's best still comes from there. Cinnamon is used in dishes ranging from milk puddings to pickles, and is essential in spice blends such as garam masala.

COCONUT MILK/CREAM
Not to be confused with the juice found inside a coconut (coconut water), coconut milk/cream is the liquid obtained by pressing the grated flesh of a coconut. Traditionally, water is used in the process, with each subsequent pressing (up to three) producing a thinner milk. In countries where coconut milk is used on a daily basis, the various pressings have specific uses in cooking — a much more sophisticated use than we can get from the tinned variety. However, it is still worth shopping around for the best — coconut milk should have a clean, white colour, with the heavier cream on top, and a pleasant flavour free of aftertaste.

CORIANDER (CILANTRO)
Native to southern Europe and the Mediterranean, coriander is an essential element in curries. Fresh and dried coriander are quite

different, and of the fresh plant, the leaves, stem and root can all be used. The roots are used in curry pastes and sauces: the stems when a strong coriander flavour is needed, and the leaves are added at the end of cooking, for flavouring and to garnish. Fresh coriander is fragrant with a gingery edge, while the dried seeds have a sweeter, slightly peppery aroma.

CURRY LEAVES

Shiny, dark green curry leaves are from a tropical evergreen tree native to Sri Lanka and India. The tree is a relative of the lemon tree, and shares its lingering citrusy, slightly spicy aroma. Fresh curry leaves are used widely in southern Indian, Sri Lankan and Malay cooking. When added whole to dishes, the leaves are first cooked in oil to extract their aroma and distinct flavour, then discarded at the end and not eaten. They are also used as a garnish. Fresh leaves should be kept in the refrigerator. If buying dried leaves, choose ones that have retained their green colour.

EGGPLANT (AUBERGINE)

This tropical Asian fruit comes in an array of shapes, sizes and colours. The popular varieties include long, skinny, pale green ones — similar to purple Japanese baby eggplants, but milder — as well as Thai apple eggplants (confusingly, the size of golf balls), which are full of seeds and can be quite bitter. Other varieties are the sour-tasting fuzzy eggplants and pea eggplants. This last type grows in clusters and is bitter-tasting, but is valued precisely for that quality. They are sometimes available pickled in jars.

FIVE-SPICE

Five-spice originated in China and contains ground star anise, fennel seeds, cassia or cinnamon, Szechuan pepper and cloves. As with all spice blends, proportions vary depending on the cook, though generally the star anise dominates. In some versions, five-spice is not five at all but six- or seven-spice — ginger and/or cardamom may sneak in. This blend is pungent and quite potent, so a little goes a long way. It is used in marinades for meat, fish or poultry.

GINGER

Ginger is used extensively in Chinese, Indian and Asian cooking for its sweet aroma and peppery, tangy flavour. It is featured in soups, curries and salads, and in relishes for its clean, digestive qualities. When buying, look for plump examples with pink-beige skin. The flesh inside should be moist and creamy-lemon. Ginger is also available dried, ground and pickled.

LIME

Wonderfully tangy and aromatic, lime are native to the tropics. They are valued as a souring agent and are added to innumerable curries and stews and are particularly good in dipping sauces, chutneys and pickles. It is not difficult to make your own lime pickles, but ready-made pickled limes are easily bought from Asian food stores. To get the maximum flavour impact from fresh limes, squeeze them only as needed — for this reason, too, the juice is generally added to a dish only at the end of cooking.

MINT

Throughout its culinary history, mint has been used with remarkable consistency — that is, with meat, particularly lamb, in drinks and in sauces and pickles. It appears in cold and hot drinks, salads, chutneys, raitas and desserts — as well as the occasional curry. In countries, where much of the food is hot and spicy, mint is greatly valued for its cooling properties and sweet, light flavour. There are many local varieties of mint, but common garden mint is a fine substitute. Buy fresh leaves and store for up to a week in the refrigerator, or tightly seal in a bag and freeze.

TAMARIND

The tropical tamarind tree is prized for its fruit pods, each containing a sticky, fleshy acidic pulp wrapped around small, shiny, dark-brown seeds. It's pulp is greatly appreciated for its refreshing sweet–sour taste and fruity aroma. It serves as an excellent souring agent, and is used in soups, curries, chutneys, drinks and sweetmeats. Tamarind is sold as a concentrated paste in jars, or in blocks or cakes that still contain the seeds. Store both in the refrigerator for up to 1 year.

INDEX

A

almonds
  chicken, almond and
    raisin curry 152
  Indian pork, honey and
    almond curry 154
  spiced chicken with
    almonds 110
apricots, chicken curry with
  175

B

Balinese seafood curry
  84
Balti-style lamb 101
barbecue duck curry with
  lychees 151
beef
  beef and mustard seed
    curry 57
  beef balls with pickled
    garlic 90
  beef rendang 48
  Massaman beef curry 37
  Sri Lankan pepper beef
    curry 45
  Thai basil, beef and
    green peppercorn
    curry 125
  Thai beef and peanut
    curry 14
  Thai beef and pumpkin
    curry 176
  Thai red beef curry
    with Thai eggplants 26
bhajis, onion curry 62
bitter melon, pork curry
  with 96
breads 58-61, 183
Burmese chicken curry
  46
butter chicken 37

C

chapati 183
Chiang Mai pork curry
  179

chicken
  Burmese chicken curry
    46
  butter chicken 37
  chicken, almond and
    raisin curry 152
  chicken and Thai apple
    eggplant curry 42
  chicken curry with
    apricots 175
  chicken masala 147
  Indonesian chicken in
    coconut milk 119
  Malaysian chicken curry
    64
  Malaysian Nonya
    chicken curry 86
  rich chicken koftas 28
  spiced chicken with
    almonds 110
  spicy chicken and
    tomato curry 136
  Thai green chicken curry
    120
  Vietnamese mild chicken
    curry 170
chutneys
  coconut and coriander
    chutney 186
  fresh coconut chutney
    186
coconut
  coconut rice 182
  duck and coconut curry
    103
  fresh coconut chutney
    186
  Indonesian chicken in
    coconut milk 119
creamy prawn curry
  113
cucumber and tomato
  raita 187
curried squid 78

D

dal 68

duck
  barbecue duck curry
    with lychees 151
  duck and coconut curry
    103
  Thai red duck curry with
    pineapple 20
dum aloo 117

E

eggplant
  chicken and Thai apple
    eggplant curry 42
  hot and sour eggplant
    curry 98
  pork curry with eggplant
    17
  Sri Lankan eggplant
    curry 76
  Thai eggplants 26, 85
  Thai red beef curry with
    Thai eggplants 26

F

fish balls, Thai green curry
  with 139
fish curry
  Goan 892
  tamarind 95
fish and peanut curry 22
fish in yoghurt curry 54
fish koftas in tomato
  curry sauce 122
five-spice pork curry 130
fresh coconut chutney
  186

G

garlic, pickled 90
Goan fish curry 89
green bananas, snapper
  with green bananas
  and mango 160
green curry paste 120
green herb pork curry
  144

H

hot and sour eggplant
  curry 98

I

Indian pork, honey and
  almond curry 154
Indian tomato oil pickle
  187
Indonesian chicken in
  coconut milk 119
Indonesian pumpkin and
  spinach curry 157

J

jungle curry prawns 70

K

Kenyan coriander lamb
  135
koftas
  fish koftas in tomato
    curry sauce 122
  rich chicken koftas 28
  spinach koftas in yoghurt
    sauce 67

L

lamb
  Balti-style lamb 101
  Kenyan coriander lamb
    135
  lamb and spinach curry
    142
  lamb dhansak 51
  lamb korma 30
  lamb rizala 169
  lamb shank and yoghurt
    curry 25
  minced lamb with orange
    159
  minted lamb curry 162
  rogan josh 75
  sour lamb and bamboo
    curry 104
lentils
  dal 68

lamb dhansak   51
seasoned rice and lentils
   22
lychees, barbecue duck
   curry with   151

M
makrut (kaffir lime) leaves
   119
Malaysian chicken curry
   64
Malaysian hot and sour
   pineapple curry   93
Malaysian Nonya chicken
   curry   86
minced lamb with orange
   159
minted lamb curry   162
Massaman beef curry   37
Massaman vegetable curry
   19

N
naan   183

O
onion bhaji curry   62
orange, minced lamb with
   169

P
paneer and pea curry   132
peanuts
   fish and peanut curry
      22
   Thai beef and peanut
      curry   14
pickle, Indian tomato oil
   187
pineapple
   Malaysian hot and sour
      pineapple curry   93
   Thai red duck curry with
      pineapple   20
   Thai sweet pork and
      pineapple curry   173
pork
   Chiang Mai pork curry
      188
   five-spice pork curry   130
   green herb pork curry
      144
   Indian pork, honey and
      almond curry   154
   pork and bitter melon
      curry   96

pork and cardamom
   curry   114
pork curry with eggplant
   17
pork vindaloo   83
Sri Lankan fried pork
   curry   72
Thai sweet pork and
   pineapple curry   173
prawns
   creamy prawn curry   113
   jungle curry prawns   70
   prawns with Thai basil
      141
   scallops and prawns chu
      chee   33
   spicy prawns   52
   Thai hot and sour prawn
      and pumpkin curry   107
pumpkin
   Indonesian pumpkin and
      spinach curry   157
   Thai beef and pumpkin
      curry   176
   Thai hot and sour prawn
      and pumpkin
      curry   107

R
raita, cucumber and
   tomato   187
red curry paste   20
rice
   absorption method   166
   coconut rice   182
   rapid boil method   166
   saffron rice   182
rich chicken koftas   28
rogan josh   75
roti   184

S
saffron rice   182
scallops and prawns chu
   chee   33
seafood
   Balinese seafood curry
      84
   creamy prawn curry   113
   curried squid   78
   fish and peanut curry
      22
   fish in yoghurt curry   54
   fish koftas in tomato
      curry sauce   122
   Goan fish curry   89

jungle curry prawns
   70
prawns with Thai basil
   141
scallops and prawns chu
   chee   33
snapper with green
   bananas and mango
   160
spicy prawns   52
tamarind fish curry   95
Thai green curry with
   fish balls   139
Thai hot and sour prawn
   and pumpkin
   curry   107
snapper with green
   bananas and mango
   160
sour lamb and bamboo
   curry   104
spice blend   181
spiced chicken with
   almonds   110
spicy chicken and tomato
   curry   136
spicy prawns   52
spinach
   Indonesian pumpkin and
      spinach curry 157
   lamb and spinach curry
      142
   spinach koftas in yoghurt
      sauce   67
squid, curried   78
Sri Lankan eggplant curry
   76
Sri Lankan fried pork curry
   72
Sri Lankan pepper beef
   curry   45

T
tamarind fish curry   95
Thai basil   119, 149
Thai basil, beef and green
   peppercorn curry
   125
Thai beef and peanut curry
   14
Thai beef and pumpkin
   curry   176
Thai green chicken curry
   120
Thai green curry with fish
   balls   139

Thai hot and sour prawn
   and pumpkin
   curry   107
Thai red beef curry with
   Thai eggplants
   26
Thai red duck curry with
   pineapple   20
Thai sweet pork and
   pineapple curry   173
Thai yellow vegetable
   curry   39
tomatoes
   cucumber and tomato
      raita   187
   fish koftas in tomato
      curry sauce   122
   fresh tomato relish   138
   Indian tomato oil pickle
      187
   spicy chicken and
      tomato curry   136
turmeric   45, 58

V
vegetarian
   dal   68
   dum aloo   117
   hot and sour eggplant
      curry   98
   Indonesian pumpkin and
      spinach curry   157
   Malaysian hot and sour
      pineapple curry   93
   Massaman vegetable
      curry   19
   paneer and pea curry
      132
   spinach koftas in yoghurt
      sauce   67
   Sri Lankan eggplant
      curry   76
   Thai yellow vegetable
      curry   39
Vietnamese mild chicken
   curry   170

Y
yellow curry paste   39
yoghurt   184
   fish in yoghurt curry   54
   lamb shank and yoghurt
      curry   25
   spinach koftas in yoghurt
      sauce   67

Published in 2017 by Murdoch Books, an imprint of Allen & Unwin

Murdoch Books Australia
83 Alexander Street
Crows Nest NSW 2065
Phone: +61 (0) 2 8425 0100
Fax: +61 (0) 2 9906 2218
murdochbooks.com.au
info@murdochbooks.com.au

Murdoch Books UK
Ormond House
26–27 Boswell Street
London WC1N 3JZ
Phone: +44 (0) 20 8785 5995
murdochbooks.co.uk
info@murdochbooks.co.uk

For Corporate Orders & Custom Publishing, contact our Business Development Team at
salesenquiries@murdochbooks.com.au.

Publisher: Corinne Roberts
Project Editor: Ice Cold Publishing
Designer: Sarah Odgers
Photographer: Ashley Mackevicius
Stylist: Wendy Berecry
Food Editor: Jane Lawson
Recipe Development: Vanessa Broadfood, Vicky Harris and the Murdoch Books Test Kitchen
Production Manager: Rachel Walsh

A cataloguing-in-publication entry is available from the catalogue of the
National Library of Australia at nla.gov.au.

ISBN 978 1 760522551 Australia
ISBN 978 1 760527563 UK

A catalogue record for this book is available from the British Library.

Printed by 1010 Printing International Limited, China

IMPORTANT: Those who might be at risk from the effects of salmonella poisoning (the elderly, pregnant
women, young children and those suffering from immune deficiency diseases) should consult their doctor with
any concerns about eating raw eggs.

OVEN GUIDE: You may find cooking times vary depending on the oven you are using. For fan-forced ovens,
as a general rule, set the oven temperature to 20°C (70°F) lower than indicated in the recipe.

MEASURES GUIDE: We have used 20 ml (4 teaspoon) tablespoon measures. If you are using a
15 ml (3 teaspoon) tablespoon add an extra teaspoon of the ingredient for each tablespoon specified.